NATIONAL ANTHEMS

NATIONAL ANTHEMS

PAUL NETTL

Translated by Alexander Gode

Second, enlarged edition

FREDERICK UNGAR PUBLISHING CO.
NEW YORK

First edition 1952

Second, enlarged edition 1967

Copyright © 1967 by
Frederick Ungar Publishing Co., Inc.

Third Printing, 1975

Printed in the United States of America

ISBN 0-8044-5730-1

Library of Congress Catalog Card Number: 66-26509

The author, the translator, and the publisher

of this work

dedicate it to

the United Nations

with the proposal

that the anthem of the United Nations be

in the hope

that all peoples—

each in its own language—

devise for it a text

conceived in the spirit

in which the music was composed.

FOREWORD

This book was first conceived and written during the dark days of the second World War. In its present form it bears but scant resemblance to the original manuscript. One reason is that constant changes in the political arena kept changing facts and conditions in the field of the national anthem. This will continue to hold true while the book is on press and certainly after its publication. In this sense, then, it is obvious that the author cannot claim definitiveness or completeness or absolute up-to-date cor= rectness for his work. Yet in another sense, the golden age of the national anthem seems closed. The concept itself evolved in the Western world during the eighteenth century. Its spread and expansion to all parts of the world — as both an expression and a vehicle of modern nationalism — is essentially a phenomenon of the nineteenth century. The twentieth has produced addenda and modifications and no doubt will go on producing them. But if this means that future editions of the present work will be in need of corrections and emendations, it is also safe to assert that as a general history of national anthems the book will stand.

The author wishes to acknowledge his indebtedness to the many diplomatic and civil representatives of foreign countries in the United States who were unstinting in their readiness to answer queries and supply information (though he may note as an signifi= cant fact that in some cases answers and information failed to come forth for the simple reason that they were not available). Less formal thanks are due Mrs. Margaret Bush, Mr. Paul Mueller, and Mr. Don Sonnedecker; also Dr. Alexander Gode who is responsible for the English translation.   P. N.

vii

Translator's Note: Professor Nettl's work on the national an=
thems of the world presented the translator with a special chal=
lenge by reason of its numerous textual quotations. Existing
English renderings proved usable in only one or two instances.
The perfect translation of texts of this kind is hard to accomplish
though easy to describe: it should be faithful in rhyme and rhythm
and yet as literal as possible in point of fact and thought; but
above all, it should be poetically neither worse nor better than the
original. In some instances the translator fell short because the
task before him could only be solved by a real poet; in other cases
he did not achieve the ideal because the involuntary humor of
gloriously bad poetry seems even harder to preserve in translation
than things of verbal beauty. He did his best and takes this
opportunity to admit that he is not displeased with his translations
from languages akin to English. As for the others, they vary in
merit; some proved impossible, and the translator thought it but
honest not to conceal that fact.

Since the publication of the first edition of this work, the author
and the translator of it have grown older by fifteen years and have
become fast friends. During this time, the number of nations with
national anthems has almost doubled, and the second edition of
this work is considerably longer than the first. Basically, however,
little has changed in the field of national-anthems. Professor Nettl
sees no need for a new introduction, and the translator, confirmed
in what he said in his original Note, reports with delight that his
remarks on the difficulty of preserving in translation the involuntary humor of gloriously bad poetry have been quoted repeatedly.

A. G.

CONTENTS

NATIONAL ANTHEMS

NATIONALISM AND MUSIC

Love of country has always been among the strongest of man's impulses. Nationalism and patriotism are a sort of collective self-confidence. The pride a man takes in his noble descent or in his personal work corresponds in another sphere to the pride he takes in being a member of his nation and the love he feels for his country. National self-confidence is often an overcompensated national inferiority complex expressed in men's inclination to overrate their own people. This is particularly the case with nationalities lacking in inner equilibrium, as for instance the Germans, the Czechs, the Poles, and the Jews, that is, in other words, with most nations of a turbulent historical past.

The correspondence between the pride which individuals take in their families' past and the national and patriotic fervor of races and peoples is further highlighted by the common fact that nations trace their origins to prehistoric events, enshrined in legends and myths of heroes and gods. The Jews link the beginnings of their history to the One God, and the origins of the ancient Greeks and Romans are likewise rooted in mythology.

As Vergil sang in the Aeneid, the founding of Rome is ascribed to the Trojan Aeneas — son of Venus, son-in-law of Priamus — who succeeded in escaping the gory massacre which the Achaeans inflicted upon his native city and who — after prolonged wander=ings — reached Italy where he laid the cornerstone of the majestic structure which came to be the later Roman Empire.

The British — or at least some of them — are convinced that they are the descendants of the "chosen people" of the Old Testament. Milton stated that his people was created to bring the light to others, to live in freedom, and to glorify Christ; and legend has it

1

that the twelve dispersed tribes of Israel are identical with the Anglo-Celtic peoples. There actually was an *Anglo-Israel Identity Society* dedicated to the task of proving that the British of today are the grandchildren of the old Israelites. They are the "chosen people" of modern times, and are called upon to rule all other nations. The first modern apostle of this society was one Richard Brothers (1757–1824), the "nephew of the Almighty," as he called himself. He had learned that he was a descendant of David and prophesied that he would be revealed as Prince of the Hebrews on November 19, 1795. About that time he was committed to Newgate and later to a lunatic asylum where he was kept till 1806: These ideas became fairly widespread in the nineteenth century when Queen Victoria, likewise "a descendant of David," was expected to fulfill the prophecy that the "line of David shall rule for ever and ever" (Chron. II).

This is one illustration in lieu of many. Others might be drawn from the popular histories of Venice, Switzerland, Denmark, Bohemia, and any number of countries which trace their origins to gods and heroes — a fact undoubtedly connected with men's desire to believe, and to have others believe, that their nation was the first to appear on this globe and hence is the one that may right= fully claim the first place in the sun.

Men's preoccupation with the origin of their people and the pride they take in the heroic descent of their clan have a close correspondence in the idea that the nation to which one belongs must have a special mission in the life of all mankind. The Jews got the assignment to spread the belief in One God among the Gentiles. The Romans considered it their special task to permeate the world with Roman customs and Roman law. The French of the Revolutionary era felt called upon to spread among nations the ideas of equality and brotherliness, and the German National Socialists, preaching the doctrine that under German hegemony the world should be converted to National Socialist ideas, adopted as their slogan the couplet of the poet Geibel,

Und es mag an deutschem Wesen
Einmal noch die Welt genesen.

(In the end through German force
comes redemption to man's course.)

It is Switzerland's mission to show the world how several nationalities — compressed within narrow territorial confines but without the link of close traditional affinities — can associate in an intimate symbiosis if they are inspired by principles of democ= racy and peace.

It is the mission of contemporary Russia to acquaint the world with the blessings of Communism while people in the United States dream hopefully of spreading the democratic gospel.

So it is that faith in the superiority of one's people is one of the sturdiest roots of patriotism. Another element in it is love of home and country, an emotion apt to come to the fore most strongly when a man's life has taken him to distant parts. Homesickness can be a very profound experience. Modern psychology sees in back of men's love for their homeland an identification in their emotional subconscious of soil and mother; hence the expression "Mother Earth." The earliest childhood impressions, which later life cannot obliterate, are of crucial significance in the development of a man's character. They all — and among them the land and the people of his earliest environment — appear in a sense as part and parcel of his adult personality. Language and reason, speech types and thought, are largely determined by a subject's native region.

It is known that the sound of an alpenhorn will arouse such homesickness in Swiss or Tirolese emigrants that they resolve right there and then to return to the land of their yearning. In past centuries, Swiss soldiers enlisted in foreign armies would often desert under the spell of homesickness when listening to a *ranz des vaches*. For this reason Swiss guards and mercenaries were at times forbidden to sing their folksongs. There is a whole string of Swiss "songs of yearning," as for instance the Strasbourg song:

3

Zu Straßburg auf der Schanz
Da ging mein Trauern an.
Das Alphorn hört' ich drüben anstimmen,
Ins Vaterland wollt' ich hinüberschwimmen,
Das ging ja nicht an.

(On Strasbourg's ramparts strong
My sad fate was drawn on.
The alpenhorn I heard on yon side beginning.
To my homeland I tried to flee swimming.
I should not have gone.)

The melody of this folk song which stems from the eighteenth century — the original having been recorded in Hesse-Darmstadt in 1786 — inspired Gustav Mahler in the composition of his famous song in which all his melancholy longing is so perfectly expressed.

Under Rousseau's influence, the Alpine herdsman enjoyed great popularity as the subject of romantic enthusiasm, and so did the *ranz des vaches*, already brought into vogue through the publica=tion of Zwingerus-Hoferus' *Dissertatio Medica Tertia: De Potho=patridalgia* (Basel, 1710), which contains what is probably the earliest medical description of homesickness.

One of the characteristic features of the *ranz des vaches* or *Kuhreihen* is the augmented fourth, the so-called "alpenhorn fa" which is the eleventh harmonic. Under its spell we can well imagine that the sound of the alpenhorn had the effect described in Zwingerus-Hoferus' scholarly dissertation.

The widespread enthusiasm for the *ranz des vaches* was further emphasized by Rousseau in his *Dictionnaire de musique* where he published a specimen under the title *"Air suisse appellé le ranz des vaches."* He must have heard it in his Swiss homeland. Since it is not generally known, a transcription of it (after the edition of 1768) may be inserted at this point.

4

5

Music is indeed a source of powerful emotional charges which strengthen men's attachment to their native lands. That is in no sense a startling observation. Nothing is apter than music to raise a half-consciously dormant emotion into the sphere of complete consciousness. A simple tune, a rhythmic phrase, known to us in our youth or in better and more beautiful days, may conjure up in our memory the happy hours or minutes of those days long since forgotten but now revived in sharp contour with all the indications of a profound emotional experience. Music is marvel= ously equipped to set in motion the psychic mechanism of the *déjà vu*.

The lullaby which the mother or nurse once sang to quiet the babe in arms turns out to be a powerful psychological force. Millions of people have no access whatever to poetry and music except by way of the nursery song. They judge music entirely in proportion to its kinship with children's and folk songs they know. The origin of the more complex forms of music are to be traced ultimately to primitive children's songs. In fact, poetic as well as musical rhythm is lastly based on the principle of cardial systole and diastole, the dualism of the human body, which determines the rhythm of walking, marching, and hence of dancing as well as the consequent musical forms.

This accounts for the fact that it is not possible to imagine human existence completely without music. Music and poetry are indissolubly connected with our lives; they are so connected by virtue of the bodily substance of our being into which our mothers — while bearing us in their wombs — inculcated the rhythm of their rolling gait.

Art — it goes without saying — has played at all times a tremen= dously important part in the history of patriotism. Indeed, one might say that art — and music in particular — has served as a surrogate for wealth and power in times of political and economic depressions. So the German historian of music Kretzschmar observes that the German songs and cantatas enabled the German people "to preserve in lean years their unbroken vigor of life and faith."

A striking case in point is the Austrian folk song of "*Prinz Eugenius*" (Prince Eugene of Savoy) which was written—if popular tradition can be trusted — by a soldier from Brandenburg. Accord= ing to Ferdinand Freiligrath, whose imaginative poem of the same title describes the genesis of the folk song, it was the inspiration of an Austrian trumpeter reminiscing about his experiences during the battle of Belgrade on August 16, 1716, while camping with his comrades somewhere on the Danube a week or so after the events. At any rate, the song — and also Freiligrath's poem in Carl Loewe's setting — came to be a source of inspiration for many an Austrian and German soldier. It is no great exaggeration to speak of the folk song of "*Prinz Eugenius*" as a forerunner of the Austrian national anthem.[1]

At the time when religious unrest and strife beset medieval Europe, religious songs were a primary factor in the maintenance of religious fervor and faith, and likewise — wherever faith was tinged by national endeavor, as it was, for example, in the case of the Hussites — of national pride and patriotism. When medieval flagellants appeared in an Italian or German city, their songs carried away numberless men and women who changed from curious bystanders to wholehearted participants. In exactly the same way the wild songs of the Hussites inspired their own ranks and routed their enemies.

A specific instance of religious fervor galvanizing a motley crowd into a victorious army of patriots is that of the battle of Sempach on July 9, 1386, when fifteen hundred Swiss peasants defeated an Austrian army of five thousand soldiers and killed their commander, Duke Leopold III, known as the Valiant. The battle is one of decisive importance in the long drawn-out wars which the Swiss had to wage in order to establish their independ= ence from the feudal authority of the Austrian Hause of Haps= burg. According to contemporary accounts, the Austrians attributed their defeat to the impetuosity of their youthful knights. The

Swiss, at any rate, were so overawed by their incredible success that they attributed it later on to the valor of Arnold von Winkelried, a legendary adaptation of an historical figure who seems to have played an important part in the battle of Bicocca in 1522. We are told how, at a critical moment in the battle of Sempach, when the Swiss had failed to break the serried ranks of the Austrian knights, Arnold von Winkelried, a man from Unterwalden, came to their rescue. Commending his wife and children to the care of his com= rades, he rushed towards the Austrians, gathered a number of their spears together against his breast, and fell pierced through and through, having opened a way into the hostile ranks for his countrymen.

The legend has undoubtedly great beauty and charm. But the historical facts are no less inspiring. We know, again from contem= porary sources, that before the engagement at Sempach the Austrians in deep silence heard the kneeling Swiss sing a German version of the *antiphona de morte* by the ninth-century monk, Notker Balbulus of St. Gall:

> *Media vita in morte sumus.*
> *Quem quaerimus adiutorem*
> *nisi te, domine?*
> *Qui pro peccatis nostris*
> *iuste irasceris.*

This is of course the original on which Luther based his hymn, *"Mitten wyr ym leben sind / mit dem tod umbfangen..."* The Sempach text may have been closer to what is still an integral part of the Catholic Hymnal in German-speaking lands:

> *Mitten in dem Leben sind*
> *Wir vom Tod umfangen;*
> *Wer ist's der auf Hülfe sinnt,*
> *Daß wir Gnad' erlangen?*
> *O Herr, du bist's alleine.*
> *Uns reuet unsre Missetat,*
> *Die dich, Herr, erzürnet hat.*

(In the midst of our lives
Death has us surrounded.
Who, to lead us, ever strives,
Back to Grace unbounded?
Lord of Glory, none but Thou!
We repent our evil course
Which incites Thy anger's force.)

The chroniclers make no mention of the Austrians having pre=
pared themselves for battle by singing either a battle song or a
religious hymn. We may assume that they did nothing of the sort
and conclude that the Swiss owed their victory to Notker's famous
antiphony.

Having mentioned Luther's name in the foregoing context, it
may be fitting for us to conclude these references to the inspira=
tional power of music by quoting a Jesuit writer who expressed the
opinion that the German Reformer's „A mighty fortress is our
Lord" had "played more souls into the hands of the devil than all
the Protestant pamphlets taken together."

♩♩♩♩♩♩♩♩♩♩♩♩♩♩♩♩♩♩♩♩♩♩♩♩♩♩♩♩♩♩

Political rivalry of two nations is often reflected in the sphere of
music. The question as to which music was better, the French or
the Italian, provoked in seventeenth and eighteenth-century France
numerous hotly contested discussions. It is a strange fact that it
was an Italian — G. B. Lully — who founded the national French
opera. Musical nationalists, to be sure, have tried to deny him this
honor in favor of the Frenchman, Robert Cambert. When Casanova
saw at the Paris Opera a French ballet in which a "Dance of the
Venetian Doges" occurred, we may suspect that it was his partisan
pride which prompted him to find the whole performance "utterly
ridiculous." It was no doubt for similar reasons that he felt terribly
bored when he heard what he called "the dreary recitatives" of
the opera, *les Fêtes vénitiennes* by Campra. When a French aria
made him yawn, a Frenchman occupying the same box explained

9

to him that he — the Frenchman — had almost died with boredom at the opera in Italy, and this in turn produced a veritable eruption of Italian patriotism on the part of the famous Venetian adven= turer. In such matters it is fairly dangerous to take sides, but the impartial historian must record the fact that from the seventeenth to the beginning of the nineteenth century everybody in Europe recognized the supremacy of Italian music and furthermore that France did in truth profit from Italian music in her own national interest. After Lully, it was, next to the German Gluck, the Italian Cherubini — followed later on by the German Jews Meyerbeer and Offenbach — who determined the characteristically national traits of French music.[2]

National trends and rivalries in the realm of music have not always kept within peaceful bounds. The appearance of an Italian opera company in Paris in 1752 brought about the world-famous quarrel of the "bouffonists and anti-bouffonists." The former, that is, the partisans of the Italian *opera buffa* (most significantly and characteristically represented by Pergolesi's *Serva Padrona*), were predominantly members of the Parisian intelligentsia, while some members of the royal family, and with them both the aristocracy and the plutocracy, upheld the interests of the French national opera. While the king and Mme de Pompadour favored the French national opera, the queen sided with men like Rousseau, Diderot, d'Alembert, and Baron Grimm in their preference for Italian music. Here we actually have a case where the field of music was the arena in which occurred the clash of two worlds separated by social and cultural antagonisms. And indeed, the encounters — which were fought out in the press, in salons, and boudoirs — were nothing if not embittered.

In this connection we must bear in mind that the philosophers, Rousseau ahead of them all, stood for the world of the future, that is, a democratic world which aspired simultaneously toward a new kind of music. The older music of France was representative of royalism and aristocracy while the Italian *opera buffa* and the German symphony could be identified with the bourgeoisie.

In his fight for a simplified, back-to-nature sort of music, Rousseau produced his intermezzo *le Devin du village* (1752) which had considerable importance for the development of both the *opéra comique* and the German *singspiel*. The *opéra comique* and the operetta with their rural themes represent the coming third estate, while the German *singspiel* — equally conditioned by Rousseau and the English ballad opera — prepared the emancipation of German dramatic music from the Italian opera. Indeed, this intimate association of social and national endeavors with musical problems has never been adequately stressed. Actually we hear in this seemingly harmless battle of the bouffonists and anti-bouf= fonists the distant rumbling of revolutionary thunders.

Twenty years later a similar encounter took place in Paris. This time the adherents of the Italian opera gathered around Niccolò Piccini while the forces of French tradition rallied under the banner of the German Gluck. No one foresaw that this man's work would eventually form the basis of a German, in any event, of an emi= nently national musical movement which was to attain its goal in the music drama of Richard Wagner.

In another context we shall have occasion to discuss the uprising of musical nationalists in Berlin against the foreigner Spontini, an affair which culminated in an unbelievable theatrical scandal during the performance of Mozart's *Don Giovanni* in 1841.

At the Viennese music and drama expositon of 1892, Smetana's *Bartered Bride* had its first performance outside Bohemia. This event aroused the national feelings of the German student body who tried to stage major anti-Czech demonstrations but could not prevent the performance from becoming a huge success for the Czechs whose musical genius was being discussed all over the world.

Smetana's operas and symphonic works — especially *My Father= land (Má Vlast)*, the operas *Libussa, Dalibor,* and *The Branden= burgers in Bohemia* — have done more than anything else to awaken the national consciousness of the Czechs. As a matter of fact, music has always played a major part in the conflict of the Czechs

11

and Germans in Bohemia. A symbol of this situation may well be seen in the *Ständetheater* in Prague which dates from the eighteenth century and is the place where the first performance of Mozart's *Don Giovanni* was given on October 29, 1787. As long as Bohemia was a part of the Austro-Hungarian monarchy, the performances at the famous theater on Caroline Square were given in German; with the advent of the Czechoslovak Republic they were continued in Czech. Under the Nazis the *Ständetheater* was a symbol of German art, and after the expulsion of the Germans on May 5, 1945, it served equally well as a symbol of Czech art.

The endeavor of the Czechs to develop their own national music was unique in its passionate singleness of purpose. When the Czech national theater — the scene of the first nights of Smetana's and Dvořák's operas—was destroyed by fire, the people as a whole raised penny upon penny until the sum required for a new building was on hand. German music was at first excluded from the repertoire. In course of time it came at least to be tolerated although only slowly and quite reluctantly. A performance at the Czech national theater of the opera *Wozzek* by Alban Berg, shortly before Hitler s invasion, was the occasion of a big scandal. The demonstrations were directed not so much against the opera as such but rather against things German in general and also, it is true, against the possibility of a leftist influence in cultural matters.[3]

In Poland too we find the most intimate association of national= ism with music. As far back as the sixteenth century we find Polish melodies and rhythms in the works of German composers. Bach, Handel, and Telemann wrote polonaises, and the popular collection, *Die singende Muse an der Pleiße (The Muse of Song on the Pleisse River)*, which was in vogue all over Germany, bears witness to the musical expansion of a nation whose political life was at the mercy of its neighbors to the West and East. When Poland lost its independent statehood altogether, the expansive vigor of its music increased, and it was Chopin's music with its fiery rhythms whose elegiac, yet simultaneously revolutionary character won the hearts of the Parisians for the cause of Poland.

Similarly the expansive power of Bohemian music was partic=
ularly strong in the eighteenth century, that is, at a time when
the Czech nation was totally helpless under the yoke of the
Hapsburgs. Its natural affinities had been Protestant, but the
Catholic counterreformation had overwhelmed it doing away with
the last vestiges of its political and national independence. Then
the musical potentialities of the people began to move bringing
about a rarely witnessed "musification" of national life. In his
volume, *The Present State of Music in Germany*, the British
contemporary Burney relates how (in 1773) he found music to be
practiced in every home in Bohemia and how it was taught
intensively in every school in the country.

This was indeed a period during which Bohemia was so filled
with music that, as it were, a good deal of it spilled over. A veri=
table exodus of music began, for all the musical talent which the
country produced could not possibly be consumed at home. It was
then that the orchestras throughout Europe were overcrowded with
Czech musicians. A case in point is the famous Mannheim School
whose leader, Johann Stamitz, developed a new style, a new tone
language of rhythmic and melodic full-bloodedness, in sharp
contrast to the tone language of the baroque, that is of Bach,
Handel, Rameau, and others. Stamitz initiated a new symphonic
style which fascinated musical Paris about the year 1750. Haydn
and Mozart built further on this new style which was at least in
part based on Czech folklore.

It is truly fascinating to watch this politically dependent people,
the Czechs of the eighteenth century, exerting a tremendous musical
influence and occupying and holding key positions in the field of
music abroad. Georg Benda (1722—1795) as well as his brother
Franz Benda (1709—1786) were among those who emigrated from
Bohemia. In 1742 Georg became chamber musician in Berlin and
eight years later, court conductor at Gotha. He was one of the
pioneers of the German *singspiel*, that is to say, a significant factor
in the national history of German music, while his brother Franz

became one of the most highly esteemed German violinists. And the careers of both were by no means exceptional.

The problem of nationalism and music plays an exceptionally striking part in the history of Italian music and characteristically enough, especially in the history of the most Italian of all art forms, the opera. We have mentioned the Italo-French opera quarrels in a previous passage. Throughout the seventeenth and eighteenth centuries French music — not differing in this from German and English music — was constantly on the defensive against an all-pervading Italian influence. Yet the Italians — then the most musical people in Europe — were politically weak and far from united. Here again it is difficult not to suspect a causal relationship be= tween political weakness and musical strength. And indeed, there seems to be ample evidence to support the generalization that the musical expansion of a people is in the inverse ratio of its political expansion.

During the seventeenth century and far into the eighteenth century most German orchestras were dominated all but completely by Italian musicians. And so were the world-famous court or= chestra at Vienna, the orchestra of the Netherlands, the Polish and Russian court orchestras, and — most strikingly — the opera of London. Composers, conductors, singers, and dancers were almost always Italians. Bologna and Milan were theater marts with voices and talents as their stock in trade.

The fact that German, French, and English musicians and lovers of music were forced into the defensive produced the most varied symptoms. In Britain an energetic national reaction against Italian music began to make itself felt as early as the beginning of the eighteenth century. By about 1730, Handel held sway over the London opera. His quarrel with Bononcini as well as the numerous squabbles of the Italian prima donnas — the most famous being the Cuzzoni-Hasse exchange of fisticuffs on stage — had promoted a national movement which succeeded in paralyzing the Italian operatic influence for a long time. Counterbalancing the Italian opera there now arose a nationally English opera, the ballad opera, in which the great Italian coloratura arias were replaced by songs of such popular appeal that everybody knew them and was able to whistle and hum them by himself.

The most famous ballad opera, the one that initiated the entire English movement, was John Gay's *Beggar's Opera*. It ridiculed in its delightfully frivolous way not only the grand style of the Italian opera but also the aristocracy and contemporary social conditions. And here again we are confronted with the interesting fact that the protagonist of a national movement was a foreigner. The composer of the *Beggar's Opera*, this first popular English opera, was by no means an Englishman but a German — a native of Berlin whose name was Johann Christoph Pepusch. Thus the battle of the Italian opera was fought out in England by two non-Britishers, the Germans Handel and Pepusch, exactly as the interests of French music were represented in France by the German Gluck and later on by Meyerbeer and Offenbach.

In Germany the reaction against the Italian opera is characterized by countless feuds at the courts, often fought out behind the scenes, and by the endeavor to promote a German national opera in the form of the *singspiel*. It was a slow and arduous development which led in course of time to the victory of native musicians in Vienna, Dresden, Munich, and other musical centers in German lands. This held true particularly in regard to the courts.

In Vienna, Mozart endeavored to put the German *singspiel* across, but how he fared we may infer from a letter he addressed on March 21, 1785, to the writer Anton Klein. He complained bitterly about the lacking patriotism in the field of the opera and continued: "If just one single patriot's name were among those posted . . . It seems indeed that it would be an eternal blot on Germany's honor if we Germans were to begin seriously to think and act and talk German and even — to sing German! Do not hold it against me, my dearest Privy Councillor, if I have gone too far in my eagerness. Fully convinced that I was speaking to a German man, I gave my tongue a free rein, a thing which one may allow to occur so rarely these days that it seems meet and fitting after such an outpouring of one's heart that one should get joyously drunk without the risk of — harm to one's health."

Mozart did actually put into practice his precepts about a German opera. After the *Entführung* he wrote his last and possibly greatest work, the *Zauberflöte* or *Magic Flute*, thus laying the foundation for the German opera of the nineteenth century whose stages are represented by the names of Weber, Marschner, Lortzing, Nicolai, and finally Wagner. Again, it is perhaps no accident that Germany's great classical music had its heyday at a time of political disruption, when — as was the case when Haydn and Beethoven flourished — the country had reached the extremes of its political decline. Perhaps one may venture to suggest that during that period the Germans needed their music more than ever before or after. It was during his country's most tragic humiliation in the political sphere that Haydn wrote the Austrian national anthem. He glorified Austrian music through his symphonies and oratorios which proved to have greater appeal in England than in his country.

Here we may note in passing, that England, from the seventeenth century on, that is, from the time when its position as a great political power began to consolidate itself, never ceased to import German and Italian music. Beethoven wrote many of his greatest works when the political fortunes of his country had reached an all-time low. During the nineteenth century, it is true, German music, represented by names like Mendelssohn, Schumann, and Brahms, underwent a development whose final fruition in Wagner's work coincided with the period of Germany's political coming of age and her victory in 1871.

The development of Italian music in the nineteenth century is similarly parallel to Italy's struggle for unification finally consummated in the coronation of King Victor Emanuel. Verdi's part in this process is both characteristic and symbolic. The letters of his name spelled out the slogan of the *risorgimento*, *Vittore Emanuele Re d'Italia*, and were for a long time in use as such.

The Italians ruled the world musically from the seventeenth to the beginning of the nineteenth century, a period — we may note once again — when Italy was politically disrupted and weak. It seemed obvious and everybody knew that the Italian opera was in no sense a national peril, for all these kings, emperors, heroes, and gods, these princesses, goddesses, sorceresses in lovers' gardens, nymphs, and fairies appeared only on the stage and were im= personated by prima donnas and eunuchs. But these gods and kings, these goddesses and sorceresses spoke so bombastic and turgid a language, they trilled their coloraturas, whispered their oaths of love, roared their threats of death that a naive listener could often be truly and profoundly scared. Is it too bold to suggest that these Caesars and Neros, these gods of war, these condottieri and shrewd diplomats on the Venetian and Neapolitan stage were harmless surrogates and in a sense true precursors of Mussolini? We do have written accounts from the England of the time of the *Beggar's Opera* which accuse Italian music of having, through its sweet melodiousness, a slackening and enervating effect on Albion's courageous heart, pervading it with Italian weakness and de= cadence. And worse than that, Italian music was held to be a direct threat to Britain's vital hold on Gibraltar which people in their current effeminacy thought of giving back to the Spaniards. These and similar worries will be found expressed in Caleb d'An= vers, *The Craftsman*, published in London in 1731.

Italian music encountered little resistance on the Iberian pen= insula, and it is certainly not without significance that almost all the national anthems of the South American countries throughout the nineteenth century adapted the style of the Italian opera. The phenomenon of a national reaction against foreign music is naturally to be observed predominantly in times of war or national tension, and the propagandistic value of music has at all times been fully appreciated.

During World War I, German music was ostracized in England and America. In America this trend was so pronounced that Ger= man conductors, as for instance Karl Muck, did not escape being banned. For years Beethoven and Wagner disappeared from con=

17

cert programs, and after the war a *Beethoven Association* had to be organized for the purpose of reintroducing the German master to the American public. In Germany and Austria, Italian as well as French music was outlawed.

World War II was fought out without musical nationalism. Bach, Beethoven, and Brahms were performed in America and England rather more, than less, than in Germany. The reason for this peculiarity may have been that this war was widely felt to be no war among nations but rather a war of ideologies. Both in America and England great pains were taken to point out time and again that the great masters of German classical music expressed in their works the ideas of humanity, freedom, and brotherliness, as Mozart did in the *Magic Flute* or Beethoven in *Egmont* or the *Ninth* with its basic theme of *"alle Menschen werden Brüder."* The anti-Christian doctrine of the Nazis was as much at odds with the church music of the greatest German masters as with the pro= duction of foreign composers. Actually, if the Nazis could have decided these things in keeping with their principles, very little classical German music would have been performed in Germany. There was also the fact that the elimination of Jewish composers in Germany induced England and America to show themselves unusually partial to Mendelssohn and Mahler as long as the Nazi wars went on.

In America, political trends and events are often mirrored in musical attitudes. After World War I, the Finnish composer Jan Sibelius enjoyed here the greatest respect. Press and radio did their best to promote his symphonies, and it seems quite possible to find at least one of the reasons for their attitude in the fact that Finland was the only country that fulfilled its American obligations under the reparations arrangements. When Finland sided with the enemies of the Allies, Sibelius went into an eclipse. Then the Soviet composers Shostakovich and Prokofiev were the "great" foreign composers enjoying a correspondingly great popularity. But they too were granted the privilege of greatness only as long as Russia was idolized as a great ally. When the Soviet Union began to make trouble, the Shostakovich vogue abated somewhat. It is similarly to be surmised that the roots of the popularity of South American music were not unrelated to Washington's good-neighbor policies.[4]

In the case of the U.S. it is clearly correct to speak of musical expansionism. For the last thirty years or so jazz has been broad= cast to all parts of the globe and it cannot be gainsaid that it has been of considerable influence on modern music everywhere. The Frenchmen Satie, Milhaud, Honegger, the Germans Hindemith, Weill, Schulhoff, Křenek, and the Russian Stravinsky—to mention but a few — were under the influence of this typically American style of music. Beyond this the American jazz bands and negro singers with their spirituals as also the great American choirs have done their bit to spread American musical values and to dissolve the vestiges of an American national inferiority complex in regard to music. America has its musical "attachés" in foreign parts. Politics and music are more closely interrelated than may be apparent at first blush.

The question arises as to what national characteristics there are in music. A trained ear may recognize immediately whether a given melody is German or French, Spanish, Norwegian, or Hungarian. There is no doubt but what there are pronouncedly national styles in the realm of musical art forms as well. There is no doubt but what we can hear the typically German elements in Wagner's music, the typically French elements in Gounod or Bizet; we call Rossini and Verdi typically Italian and sense that Smetana and Dvořák are typically Czech.

The various psychological "types" — as differentiated by the singing teacher Rutz and taken over by Professors Sievers and Becking — can well be recognized in the music of various peoples. The idealism of the Germans which has always pervaded their politics and national culture is likewise representative of the spirit of their music. In contrast to the Frenchman who is a realist and rationalist, the German views the world in non-real ideas. He refuses to grant recognition to realities and is always ready to try to change the world. In the last analysis the Hitler catastrophe too is an expression of this spiritual trait of the Germans. In his melody and rhythm the German displays a certain "weightedness". One has the impression that he sees before him the task of displacing something which offers resistance. Often a German melody will seem to appeal nostalgically to remoteness and distance; it seems, as it were, to listen into itself. It is often immersed in sentiment, but always as though some weight were to be overcome.

The Italian, on the other hand, is lighter, less impeded by in= hibitions; he carries his weight on wings. At times he fails to heed the transition from pathos to bombast; his sentiment is a matter of form; it seems to remain on the surface and rarely penetrates the depths below.

In French music the situation is quite similar. Its floating rhythms reveal the grace and the temperament of the French. The musical language of the time of Lully reflects precisely the intellectual climate of the century of Louis XIV with its slogan *amour et gloire*.

Yet it is a remarkable fact that the major musical nationalities — let us say the Germans, the Italians, and the French — are harder to keep apart than the Russians, Czechs, Scandinavians, Hungar= ians, Spaniards, and the off-shoots of the last-named, the South American peoples.

In countries located on the periphery of the European continent — that is to say, in Scandinavia, the Slavic lands, and the Iberian peninusula — there is a much stronger influence of folk music on art music than holds true for the centrally situated countries. This may be due to the fact that folk music among the peripheral peoples remained unaffected by art music much longer than was the case with the central peoples. Dvořák's and Smetana's music, the music of Albeniz and Granados, or of Musorgski, Glinka, Borodin, and other Russians, is clearly seasoned with the aroma of their peoples' folk music.[5]

In many instances there is to be discerned an influence of the language, its particular melody and rhythm. The language of the Czechs for instance — rich in consonants and uttered in staccato style — is clearly to be recognized in Dvořák's and Smetana's Czech dances. Seemingly so unrelated a point as to whether a language possesses an article or not is reflected in music. The Czech language which has no article corresponds to the music of the Czechs which has few anacruses and a rhythm characterized by marked theses. But this fiery rhythm, about which there is something revolution= ary, does not imply that the Czechs should not also have many sentimentally lyrical songs. Their national anthem would be enough to correct such a misapprehension. It is a characteristic observation that the Poles and the Czechs whose languages owe their trochaic character to the missing article should have national dances like the mazurka and the polka, both of which have a thetic stress within the measure, while the Germans whose language does have an article developed the anacrustic waltz.

In British and Scottish folk songs, the numerous two-syllable words with a pronounced stress on the initial syllable are parallel= ed by melodies with frequent short or long appoggiaturas, brief phrases, and a clearly timed rhythm with staccato preponderance. On the other hand, the Germans and French whose languages have mute and unstressed finals are rich in melodies with longer phrases of greater uniformity and softer rhythm.

♪♪♪♪♪♪♪♪♪♪♪♪♪♪♪♪♪♪♪♪♪♪♪♪♪♪♪♪♪♪♪♪/

However charged with and expressive of national vitality, melodies and musical traits are not tied to their country of origin. The number of international and migrating melodies is immense. In a night club in Trieste or Naples you hear an Italian folk tune and a few months later you come across it a second time when it appears — syncopated and jazzed up — in the garb of a rumba or jitterbug's favorite on Broadway in New York or in Rio or Buenos Aires. The simpler and more directly comphrehensible a melody is, the more "familiar" will it appear; the more quickly will it be accepted by the world at large; the more assuredly and safely will it travel abroad, through deserts, over mountains, and across oceans.

Never before in history have music and the dance been so international as they are today. Gershwin's *An American in Paris* is as well known in Paris and Berlin as Shostakovich's *Fifth* is in London and New York or as Lehar's waltzes are in China. What is going on, is truly the most amazing long-range barter of melodies and dances.

Yet how should one try to fathom the psychological bases of this phenomenon of circulation? No song anywhere in the world has been vaster in spread and range than "Silent Night." And yet, Franz Gruber, the composer of it, was a poor country school= teacher who invented that "melody for the millions" in a secluded mountain village in Austria. Without being aware of it, he just had the right feeling for the psychology of the song hit.

For the past two centuries it has been the consensus throughout the English-speaking world that "For he is a jolly good fellow" should be regarded as song hit number one. Its melody was sung with the Marlborough text. The great English general and victor of the battle of Malplaquet against the French in 1709, John Churchill Duke of Marlborough was so feared by the French that when the false rumor of his death was spread, the French in their camp at Quesnay celebrated the occasion in a spontaneous out= burst of jubilation. They made up a lusty little song about the death of the hated general. The speed with which this song spread all over the world was truly fantastic. It was Napoleon's favorite tune, and finally it was so worn out that Goethe said he could not bear to hear it again. Yet today it is just as popular as it was two hundred and forty years ago. It is being sung in Australia as it is in China, and the Dutch in Pennsylvania use it with the text, *"Mei Pap und mei Mam waren eirisch dadrunten in Boiertown."*

It would pay to trace the earliest history of this most popular of all melodies which for awhile was considered a sort of French "National Anthem." The song whose original French version began with the words *"Marlborough s'en va-t-en guerre,"* was sung in Spain with the text *"Mambru se fuè a la guerra."* From Spain it traveled to South America where — especially in Chile — Marl=

borough was turned into Membrun. But the song is known also in Africa and Persia. The well-known Egyptologist Villoteau advanced the theory — obviously unfounded — that Napoleon's soldiers had brought it back from Africa. In Russia the song was considered typically Russian, and Rimski-Korsakov made of it (in an Oriental version) the major theme of his *Scheherazade*. We know for certain that the melody appeared in Spain as early as the sixteenth century. So the question may well be asked whether the original hero of the song was not after all Mambru instead of Marlborough, that is, not a British general but some forgotten colleague of Don Quixote's. That Mambru was replaced by Marlborough in France is not extraordinary, and Spain's close relations with the Orient are generally known. As a matter of fact, we do find in the work of the sixteenth-century folksong collector Francisco de Salinas a song, *"A cazar va Don Rodrigo,"* which has the three-tone skeleton of the Marlborough melody.

Salinas:

Marlborough:

We also encounter a very similar melody in Arabia and Syria. It is extremely old and was taken down by Idelsohn, the best-informed expert in near-eastern music.

In sum, I am inclined to believe that this most popular hit of the western world goes back to oriental beginnings; that it traveled from the Orient to Spain and thence, on the one hand, to all parts of Europe and North America and on the other to the countries of South America. No one listening to this melody in the garb of a radio commercial will suspect its fascinating antecedents.

Another instance: Everybody is familiar with the major theme of Smetana's justly renowned symphonic poem, *Vltava (Moldau)*, in which the course of this Bohemian river is described. A beauti= fully expansive theme symbolizes the peaceful current of the river. Smetana must have heard the somehow exotic melody in a region of his country east of that occupied by the Czechs, possibly from eas -Moravian or Slovak peasants. It is interesting to note that exactly the same theme is found again as number 186 of volume II in Felipe Pedrell's *Cancionero Musical Popular Español*, where it is recorded as an ancient Spanish melody. In this case too, the Spaniards may have gotten the tune from the Arabs. They forwarded it to Belgium, Poland, and South America. The Jews that were driven from Spain took it along and used it in their synagogues. They made of it the Zionist anthem, *Hatikvah*, while another adaptation of it was danced as a Polish mazurka.

The success of this global melody certainly has to do with the extreme simplicity of its tone sequence which rises from the keynote along the minor scale to its sixth and goes down again to the beginning along a simple scale. Possibly, it is an Arabic tune pattern which spread all over the world like an ancient oriental doctrine or a Persian tale.

Age-old melodies of the most primitive type are likewise to be found in the children's rhymes of all nations. Counting-out rhymes of the three and four-year olds recall through their paucity of tone the melodies of primitive tribes. So for instance the pygmoid Veddas of Ceylon have only melodies of two and three tones, just like the nursery songs of our children which are to be found all over the world. Children in all parts sing the tune of "Frère Jacques." Sixteenth and seventeenth-century Italian *bambini* sang it as is indicated by a theme which the seventeenth-century composer, Girolamo Frescobaldi, used in one of his organ works and which he called "*Fra Jacopino.*" At the time Italian children would greet (and mock) the popular but not exactly respected mendicant monks by singing after them "*Fra Jacopino*" with the age-old children's tune:

We encounter the same theme in sixteenth-century Spain where it was sung with the words, "Campania, campania." While Eng= lish, American, French, Italian, and German children sing the tune in major, the children of Poland and Russia — in keeping with the character of the east-Slavic folk song — know it in minor. In this form the song passed into the treasury of Jewish folk melodies from where Gustav Mahler took it over as the theme of his first symphony.

As previously implied, one people will not adopt the melodies of another without letting them undergo certain alterations com= mensurate with its own musical character. Let us return once again to the theme of Smetana's famous symphony. It is hardly surprising that the children of England and America should have adopted and begun to love it too. But the peoples in these countries as well as in German lands prefer a major key. That is how German children got the tune of their song, "*Fuchs, du hast die Gans gestohlen,*" which differs only slightly from the tune of "I had a little nut tree" as sung by American youngsters. Quite often we find that a traveling melody gets shortened or enlarged. In the present instance impatient children have introduced a s⌒ale with a fifth thus producing the phrase:

North American children sing with it the words, "Baa, baa, black sheep, have you any wool?" It is certainly correct to call this little song a truly international one. Mozart wrote on a similar theme his famous variations, "*Ah, vous dirai-je, maman*"; Robert Schumann — with minor changes — his "*Soldatenmarsch*"; and Beethoven the scherzo of his *Spring Sonata*.

It may be a little risky to allude here to my views on the origin of some of the melodies which we encounter in the negro spirituals. I do not know how many of them have come from Africa, but I feel reasonably certain that not a few were influenced in their current American form by Irish and Scottish melodies. This would not seem to be too surprising, for we know that many of the early settlers in the South were Irish and Scotch. Negro spirituals as well as Irish and Scottish folk songs are often built on the so-called pentatonic scale, d e g a b (d). One of the most beautiful spirituals, "Swing low, sweet chariot," was used by Dvořák in the first movement of his *New World Symphony*. In it he succeeded most admirably in rendering the peculiar mood of the American scene. A similar tune occurs in Bohemia. But what a strange causal chain! Dvořák's *New World Symphony* carried the echo of a Negro spiritual to Czechoslovakia!

Jazz themes too may at times be traced to this or that migrating melody. The well-known "Tiger Rag" is a native of New Orleans. It is an adaptation of an old French Creole quadrille and has exactly the same theme as the popular German song, "*Oh, du wunderschöner deutscher Rhein*." To be sure, the waltz of the old world appears as a foxtrot in the new.

♪♪♪♪♪♪♪♪♪♪♪♪♪♪♪♪♪♪♪♪♪♪♪♪♪♪♪♪♪♪♪

We must return once again to Spain. This strange land has, as it were, two faces. One looks toward the past and eastward, the other into the present and toward the Western Hemisphere. If it be a coincidence, it certainly is a significant one that the year 1492 marks not only the discovery of America which started from Spain but that it was in the same year that the last Moors were driven from the Iberian Peninsula. In the sixteenth and seventeenth centuries, very old Moorish songs were being sung at the port of Seville, and simultaneously the people there took up entirely new and wild dances which had been imported from the new world. It was then that the exchange of dances from one hemisphere to the other began to flourish.

Take for instance the old and venerable saraband, a dance we know so well from Bach's and Handel's keyboard music. It is one of the dances which traveled from Spain to France and spread from there all over Europe. Originally it was an unrestrained, ferocious affair, not altogether different from jitterbugging in its prime. Yet when we listen to the refined and elegiac sarabands of a Couperin or Bach, we find it hard to imagine that this should be a dance which churchmen and moralists condemned for a long period of time. The same holds true for other Spanish dances of the seventeenth century, for instance the *chaconne*[6] or the *passacaglia* and also the *folia*. All these dances are of South-American origin. In a poem, written in 1599 by Simon Agudo on the occasion of Philip II's marriage, the author suggests that one ought to go to Tampico in Mexico in order to dance the *chaconne*. And in 1618 Lope de Vega observes that this dance had come to Seville from the Indies, that is, from America:

De las Indias a Sevilla
Ha venido por la posta.

(From the Indies to Seville
It has traveled in the mail.)

Cervantes too speaks of this dance as having come from the Indies. No doubt, all these "exotic" dances had their home in the sailors' saloons of Seville, the "American" port of Spain, to where they had been brought from the Western Hemisphere. The original form of the *passacaglia* in Spain was a four-toned descending scale (*a g f e*) which even today is heard a thousand times on the guitar in Spanish lands. The old Spanish folk song, "*O guárdame las vacas*," was likewise sung after it.

27

In a travel account of 1634, the *Historia Americae* by the printer Merian of Frankfurt, I found references to the dances of the natives in the Caribbean. There is an etching of an Indian dance, and the accompanying melody shows the beginning of the same four-toned scale which is also characteristic of the early Spanish *passacaglias*. But what a change from the savage Caribbean melody to the highly civilized *passacaglias* of a Lully and a Gluck!

♪♫♪♫♪♫♪♫♪♫♪♫♪♫♪♫♪♫♪♫♪♫♪♫♪♫♪♫♪♫♪

Those brief bass motives and rhythms which characterize the Spanish dance have doubtless come from the Orient and possibly — as we have just seen — from the American colonies. The melody of the *folia*, also known as *folie d'Espagne*, is based on the motive *d c♯d e f e d*. In the eighteenth century it enjoyed a truly fabulous popularity. Every violinist is familiar with Corelli's famous varia= tions on the *folia* theme which was also used by Bach in his *Peasants' Cantata* and by Liszt in his *Rhapsodie Espagnole*. All such themes are *ostinato* themes, and it is interesting to discover a closely related element in the development of modern American dance music, that is, the "riff," a brief rhythmic figure, which the bands play over and over again while one or the other individual instrument improvises about it, quite in accordance with the old *ostinato* technique. This is the well-known Kansas City style which has left its traces in the boogie-woogie phase of jazz. It is remark= able furthermore that a goodly number of these "riff" figures consist of the same rhythmic and melodic phrases as the old *chaconnes* and *passacaglias*, that is to say, as those dances which had traveled from the Western Hemisphere to Spain. And indeed, in these *ostinato* dances we have to do with the real migrants. Embodied in them we find simultaneously Oriental, European, and American melodic material.

In seventeenth-century Italian music we find a certain bass melody called the *aria di Ruggiero* which consists of two descend= ing fifths with a corresponding conclusion ($\bar{d}$ g a d). It occurs in numerous compositions of the older period. Yet I have heard precisely the same motive used as a "riff" by a band in Harlem. Even the rhythmic variations seemed related to the old practice. Indeed, no melodic motive has roamed farther throughout Europe, Asia, and America than this one. It is also the motive which Richard Wagner used for the bells at the castle of the Grail in *Parsifal*.

Before the heyday of the cello, there lived in France a famous virtuoso on the gamba (precursor of our cello), Marin Marais. In 1701 he published a *Collection de pièces de violon* including an item called *"Carillon"*. In it we find the same motive all over again. It is of course hardly to be supposed that Wagner knew that old melody or, for that matter, any of Marais' pieces. This is simply another instance of a "migrating melody," one of those winged little things which you find everywhere and nowhere, which you pick up in the street and which, in polymorphous versatility, appear today in a rambunctious Broadway dance and tomorrow in a solemn Mass.

All these illustrations point to one conclusion, which is, that a melody — however typically representative of this or that national= ity it may be — will not necessarily remain wedded to the land of its origin. The melodies of numerous national anthems were taken over from other peoples. The most striking example is that of the British anthem which has been adopted by at least twenty different nations. The melody of the *"Marseillaise,"* too, was used as the national anthem of peoples other than the French. The national anthem of Brazil became the national anthem of Portugal; that of Austria was taken over by Germany. The British Social Demo= crats chose as their party song the melody of the German carol, *"O Tannenbaum,"* which serves likewise as the anthem of the North American state of Maryland.

The fact that the national characteristics of a given melody do not restrict it to its country of origin would seem to be at odds with the idea of specifically national traits discernible in this or that country's music. Surely, if it is correct that every nation is possessed of a specific and characteristic brand of music, it cannot but amaze us that precisely the national anthem — obviously destined to express a people's distinctive characteristics — should have been borrowed so frequently from abroad. Now it is true, there are numerous national anthems — those musically altogether typical for their respective peoples — which are hardly ever taken over by other nations. We simply cannot imagine that, let us say, the Hungarian anthem with its characteristically Hungarian phraseology could ever be adapted to serve the Spaniards or the Italians as an expression of their national fervor. The same point might be made about "Jeszcze Polska," the Polish mazurka tune which another people, for instance the Germans, could not possibly use as a national anthem. Another case in point are the hopping marches which the Italians have used by way of national anthems, so the "Inno Mameli" which became famous in 1848, the "Inno Garibaldi" (Part II) of 1859, the "Canzone di Tripoli" of 1911, the "Canzone di Piave," and the "Inno Fascista."

The typical "Yankee Doodle" will never be exported either. Yet "international" anthems — as "God save the King" and the Austrian "Gott erhalte" or even, to a lesser extent, the "Marseil= laise" — are much more objective and less dependent on autoch= thonous folklore.

The very existence of an "objective" anthem, that is, an anthem whose melody can be and has been taken over by other peoples, would seem to prove that the psychological impact of an anthem is not exclusively determined by the emotional appeal of its music. The full patriotic appeal of an anthem is determined by both the tune and the lines or — if you will — the association and rela= tionship between the two. The melody of the Prussian "Heil dir im Siegerkranz," which was taken over from the British royal anthem, assumes its complete psychological, that is, patriotic significance only if one is familiar with the lines or, at any rate, if one can conjure up the sensations and emotions which result from the association of melody and words.

♪♪♪♪♪♪♪♪♪♪♪♪♪♪♪♪♪♪♪♪♪♪♪♪♪♪♪♪♪♪♪♪♪

It is generally assumed that powerful emotions are vented in loud tones of wide intervals while more subdued feelings find expression in low sounds and narrow intervals. The intensity of a dancing or marching rhythm is similarly expressive of an elevated mood. Musicologists like Hornbostel and Curt Sachs have pointed out that peoples of markedly masculine cultures favor dances with long steps and tunes with wide intervals while peoples of a more feminine orientation in their cultures dance with short steps and use correspondingly narrower intervals. According to this theory, peoples of a warlike and adventurous spirit, being endowed with expansive powers, are apt to take to more vigorous or more compelling rhythms than do softer peoples of feminine inclinations.

It is not devoid of interest to examine a few of the more important national anthems from this point of view. The British royal anthem moves in a comparatively even rhythm and has a range of six full tones. Only once, and then just in passing, is there a range of seven full tones.

The Russian Czarist anthem was religious and introvert. It was reminiscent of church hymns and had a diatonic melody.

The Austrian imperial anthem is at first diatonic and even-structured as far as it is sung in a prayerlike mood. But where the words are emotionally charged, the intervals grow wider and the rhythm more animated. In a sense this anthem represents a connection of introvert or matriarchal and extrovert or patriarchal trends. A similar case is that of the Dutch anthem, "Wilhelmus of Nassau."

The type of anthem which is rooted in a feeling of religious devotion, is strikingly distinct from the "exalted" type which one feels tempted to characterize as aggressively imperialistic. Here we have the British anthem of expansion, "Rule Britannia," also the "Star-Spangled Banner" — regardless of the fact that the latter uses an old English melody — and especially the "Marseillaise." A typical feature of the "Marseillaise" is the arsis whose bellicose impact has been felt since the times of the ancient Greeks. The triadic tones come smashing down like thunderbolts, replete with angry enthusiasm. After six unstressed syllables there follows in the second syllable of the word *"patrie"* an emotional outburst and after the word *"gloire"* a rising and highly emphatic sixth.

This group of defiant and revolutionary anthems includes also the "Watch on the Rhine" with its clarion-like intervals and its extensive range. Its initial descending fifth expresses defiant deter= mination — there is something similar in the "Star-Spangled Banner" — while the ascending fourth of "Rule Britannia" and the *"Marseillaise"* would rather seem to represent an aggressive attitude. This rising fourth occurs likewise at the beginning of the Argentine anthem (in diatonic steps, it is true) as well as in the Italian *"Canzone di Tripoli,"* which became — with its long drawn-out "A Tripoliiiii" — Italy's most popular song.

As a general rule it may be stated that the religious and hymn-like anthems belong to an earlier age while the marching and aggressively phrased anthems appear to be more recent. The older conception of monarchy and dynasty is more adequately repre= sented by a hymn-like song while the more recent conception of revolution, expansion, and imperialism favors the fast-moving extrovert march. Almost all the anthems of the South American republics — anthems conceived in times of unrest and revolution — are marching tunes with characteristic flourishes of trumpets, and this despite the fact that they are rooted in the Italian opera of the nineteenth century. Of course, the spirit of the Italian opera does somehow correspond to the spirit of the times. After all, we must not forget that the call, *"All'armi,"* was heard a hundred times in the Venetian opera of the seventeenth century. This flourish of trumpets appears in the Italian *"Inno Garibaldi,"* precisely with the initial words, *"All' ar-mi! All' ar-mi!"*

The marching habits of the various nations as well as their attitude toward pomp and representation, toward parades and display would seem to be another factor of influence in their choice of this or that type of anthem. The rapid pace of the *Bersaglieri* has doubtless had its bearing on the Italian anthems while the slower pace of the Germans is reflected in the time of the "Watch on the Rhine." A people like the Czechs, serving against its will and under pressure in the army of the Austro-Hungarian monarchy, chose characteristically a lyrical anthem, but when the Czechs began to agitate against their oppressors, they adapted as a second anthem the revolutionary, aggressive, and strongly extrovert *"Hej Slovane"* of Polish provenance.

The emotions of patriots are changeable. What is considered sacred and sublime today, may well be despised tomorrow. National Socialism and Fascism — revered but yesterday by mil= lions as the salvation of humanity — have today been cast out by the same millions as worthless lumber. Today Communism may represent the gospel truth for millions and millions who by tomorrow may be ready to repudiate it as criminal insanity.

So it comes that national anthems — and in particular their melodies — survive their original significance. The *"Marseillaise"* has been sung by Germans fighting the French, and again the Germans sang the melody of "God save the King" in their own national anthem while striking out against the British. "Yankee Doodle" was first sung by Britishers against the Americans and then the process was reversed. The musical symbol of "Victory" used by the Allies in the second World War consisted of the first notes of Beethoven's Fifth Symphony — the sign "V" standing simultaneously for the numeral "five" and the initial letter of the word "victory." But the Germans were not slow to take up the English "victory" and make of it a German *"Viktoria."*

Thoughts, feelings, and, especially, melodies — however much their inception may be tied up with one people and one nation — are apt to go international in a very short time. In the realm of music, if anywhere, the phrase "One World" is used by rights.

GREAT BRITAIN ֊֊֊֊֊֊֊֊֊֊֊֊֊֊֊֊֊֊֊

In all the world there is no other melody as far-spread as the **British** anthem, "God save the King." It sounds like a fervent prayer. Thanks to the solemnly impressive rhythm and its well-balanced harmony, it has exerted an almost mythical attraction on a majority of the nations of this world. Even Germany, musically the richest country on earth, has taken over the tune of "God save the King" for one of its national songs. We are told that during the first World War British tommies singing "God save the King" were joined not only by Uncle Sam's doughboys whose "America" had the same tune but also by the German "field-gray youngsters" to whom it sounded familiar because it was identical with their own *"Heil dir im Siegerkranz"* ("Hail thee in victor's crown"). Early in the second World War, by the way, "Roll out the barrel" was similarly sung on both sides of the front. The Nazis claimed it as a German folk song while it was actually a product of "Tin Pan Alley."

In Germany the tune of "God save the King" was so popular that it was generally considered a German folk song. In England there is a charming anecdote about a German cook in the employ of Sir Charles Hallé, the well-known conductor and pianist. The day of her arrival in London she took a walk to see how the land lay, but when she got back to her master's home, her eyes were filled with tears of joy and gratitude, for somewhere in a park a band had played — in her honor — *"Heil dir im Siegerkranz."*

We might skip the early history of the tune — its origin is quite obscure — if it were not that during the Second World War a certain minister of the Vichy government tried once again to sell the old chestnut of its French origin. This goes back to the apocryphal

34

memoirs of the Duchess of Perth, of 1831, which (according to the German musicologist Wilhelm Tappert) were sold in London for the tidy sum of 3,000 pounds. In this source it is claimed that the text of the anthem was written by a certain Mme Brinon while the tune is said to be by Lully, the great French composer of Italian origin. Both the lines and the music, the memoirs state, were written in honor of Louis XIV who "took great delight in it" while at St. Cyr or Trianon. But lo! No other source asserts that the song ever struck root in France, except that a few royalists are known to have sung it occasionally with the words:

> Grand Dieu, sauvez le Roi,
> Grand Dieu, vengez le Roi,
> Vive le Roi!
> Que toujours glorieux
> Louis victorieux
> Voie ses ennemis
> Toujours soumis.

> (Great God, protect the King,
> Great God, revenge the King,
> Long live the King!
> That always glorious
> Lewis victorious
> May see the hostile brood
> Always subdued.)

There can be little doubt but what this is a fairly shabby trans= lation of Britain's royal anthem which French royalists of now and yesteryear felt free to adopt. The story got somehow into the memoirs of Mme de Créqui. According to Tappert, the author of the Perth memoirs "was impudent enough to include in the edition of 1840 a document signed by the mayor of Versailles in which three nuns of St. Cyr attested the veracity of the hoax about 'God save the King'." The swindle was uncovered as early as 1835. In the affair due credit must be given to a certain Perch=

eron, the executor of the Marquise de Créqui (1714—1803). This Percheron issued a statement which left no room to doubt that M. Causen (of St. Malo) — the author of the memoirs — had simply fooled the credulous world. The fable of the French origin of the British royal anthem has been disproved long since, but from time to time it is pushed to the fore again for political reasons. That was the case in 1941 when Vichy tried to exploit the matter for the purposes of its anti-British propaganda. Fifty-two years before, on September 9, 1889, the newspaper *Figaro* had served up the old hash with new trimmings. But at that time the target was not Britain but Germany whose *"Heil dir im Siegerkranz"* was viewed in France as a genuinely German national anthem. *"Guil= laume II va évidemment faire remplacer cet air national,"* read the French journal's prediction. True enough, it *was* replaced but not by William: only by Mr. Hitler.

The anthem has been ascribed to a variety of composers. The earliest name that was honored in this fashion is that of Dr. John Bull (1563—1628), who was one of the best-known British com= posers and organists of the Elizabethan era. And indeed, there is in a manuscript collection of compositions of his a piece entitled "God save the King." But this shows not the slightest resemblance to the royal anthem, although in all fairness we must hasten to add that the same collection does include an "Ayre" which exhibits at least a remote affinity with the tune we are discussing. But there is also the view that Richard Clark, sometime owner of the manu= script, may have put in a few changes without which the "Ayre" would likewise be totally different from "God save the King" as we know it.

Then there is a collection of voice compositions by Thomas Ravenscroft which appeared under the title of *Melismata* in 1611 and includes a "Carol" beginning "Remember, O thou Man." This too bears some melodic resemblance to the royal anthem although it is set in minor. Another tune that is mildly reminiscent of the anthem may be discovered in Henry Purcell's "Largo" from his Sixth Sonata of 1683.

Dr. W. H. Cummings has collected all the various theories about the origin of the melody and made a little book of them. Yet it would seem that the most acceptable view is that held by the German Handel scholar and historian of music, Friedrich Chrysander. According to him, the composer of the anthem was Henry Carey (1690—1743), in his time a very popular composer and poet of ballads and ballad operas. He was a natural son of George Savile, Marquis of Halifax. Carey is supposed to have sung the song for the first time in 1740 at a dinner given in some tavern in celebration of Admiral Vernon's victory at Portobello.

The theory that Carey composed the anthem can be traced to John Christopher Smith (Johann Christian Schmidt), the factotum and amanuensis of Handel. There is a letter written by a certain Dr. Harrington under the date line of Bath, June 13, 1795, and addressed to Carey's son. In it the writer reports that J. C. Smith, a patient of his, had assured him repeatedly that he knew for certain that Carey had written both the tune and the lines because Carey had come to see him with the melody he had just finished and had asked him to correct the bass, a favor which he — Handel's assistant, secretary, and confidant — was glad to perform.

Now, Carey was a typical song writer. Hundreds of tunes (some of traceable provenance) popped up in his fertile head, but in matters of counterpoint he did not feel completely at ease. What would be more natural than that a melody — Purcell's or John Bull's or any other for that matter — should have "occurred" to him and that it was altogether in good faith that he claimed it to be his own?

Carey died in 1743. Not much later the tune appeared in print in the collection *Thesaurus Musicus*, edited by Simpson in London. Carey's name was not mentioned. The songster and comedian, whose career had brought him neither wealth nor glory, was not at all highly reputed. Some of his compositions were brought out in careless haste for the benefit of his widow and children while the rest seemed so insignificant that no one felt inclined to pay

37

much attention to it. This "rest" may very well have included "God save the King."

As was the custom in England at the time, every melody in the collection is given twice: once for voice together with the words and again arranged for the flute which was then an extremely popular instrument. The flute arrangement as it appears in the *Thesaurus* runs as follows:

In sum then, we can only repeat that the early history of the anthem is obscure. In tracing its career, we cannot claim to be on solid ground before the year 1745 when, according to reliable sources, it was performed in two theaters — Drury Lane and Covent Garden — in arrangements by Dr. Thomas Augustine Arne, the composer of Britain's other anthem, "Rule Britannia," and his disciple, the famous historian of music, Dr. Charles Burney. The same year saw another publication of it in *Gentleman's Magazine* and also a reissue in a new edition of the *Thesaurus Musicus*.

We must remember that the song was originally a prayer for the King, who — being a German — knew English rather badly and appreciated neither Britain's culture nor its Great-Power politics, for which reasons he was bound to have numerous opponents. In 1743 he distinguished himself in the battle of Dettingen against the French; then, in 1746, he repelled the invasion of the Stuart pretender Charles Edward of Scotland. And now the song spread like wildfire all over England. There is, by the way, a theory which ascribes the melody to a Scottish composer by the name of James Oswald. There was in fact a piece referred to as "Oswald's Ayre" among the melodies played by the carillon at the parish church of Windsor, but there is no evidence whatever to prove that this was identical with "God Save the King."

The King, as everyone knows, spent as much time as possible in his native country of Hanover; and so it is not surprising that the anthem appeared very soon on the continent as well. Its first continental publication was that of 1766 in the collection, *la Lire maçonne*, which was brought out at the Hague. It is a noteworthy detail that freemasons were responsible for the transfer of the anthem to the continent. The first lodge of freemasons had been established in London in 1717, and the masonic movement spread quickly from England all over Europe. Perhaps this is the occasion to point out in passing that as early as 1731 high-ranking personages were admitted to the lodge at the Hague, specifically at the request of the British Grand Master, Lord Lovel. So, for example, Francis Stephen, Duke of Lorraine, subsequently — through his marriage to Maria Theresa — Emperor Francis I, was admitted to a masonic lodge with the assistance of British dignitaries, and it is not improbable that the royal anthem started its career on the continent as a masonic song, for the lodges were organized and presided over by Englishmen.

Dated about 1760 the tune is extant in a manuscript arrangement for the lute, last heard of as in the possession of the Germanic Museum at Nuremberg. It is, as Tappert puts it, "a very amateurish" piece of work, but it serves to show that Carey's song was known in Germany at a fairly early date.

We cannot, therefore, be surprised that in Germany too the tune was claimed to be a native product. However, this was not done officially as in Vichy-France. Only a little German schoolmaster by the name of E. Handtmann tried to prove in the *Kreuzzeitung* — number 316 of July 10, 1894 — that the tune was an adaptation of an old pilgrim's song, formerly popular in Silesia and

Moravia and still familiar as a "spring song" at the spas of Reinerz and Kudova. The words of this song are as follows:

Heil dir o Königin,
Des Brunnens Hüterin,
Heil dir, Marie.
Zum Segen und Gedeihn
Laß sprudeln klar und rein
Allzeit den Labequell.
Heil dir, Marie.

(Hail thee, o Queen, we sing,
Guardian of our spring,
Hail, Mary, thee.
For bliss and charity
Let flow in purity
Always the quenching well.
Hail, Mary, thee.)

It seems to be a fact that the British anthem was somehow con= sidered auspicious — even though the composer, Carey, spent his life in poverty and misery and ended it by his own hand. What else could explain the song's enormous attraction in all parts of the world?

The first country to adopt the anthem was apparently Denmark. In 1790, the candidate in divinity, Heinrich Harries (1762—1802), translated it rather freely into German. He had it published on January 27 in the *Flensburger Wochenblatt* under the caption, "*Lied für den dänischen Unterthan an seines Königs Geburtstag zu sin= gen*" ("Song for the Danish subject to be sung on his King's birth= day"). The first stanza reads:

Heil dir, dem liebenden
Herrscher des Vaterlands!
Heil Christian dir!
Fühl in des Thrones Glanz

Die hohe Wonne ganz,
Vater des Volks zu sein!
Heil Christian dir!

(Hail thee, o loving king,
Thou rul'st the land we own!
Hail, Christian, thee!
Feel on thy splendid throne
This joy supreme alone
To be thy people's sire.
Hail Christiar, thee.)

But, as such things are apt to do, the venture barely missed
leading to the most unpleasant surprises for the poet. Being a good
Bible student, Harries had handled one stanza as a free adaptation
of King David's Psalm XXXIII, 16 and 17, which reads, "There is
no king saved by the multitude of an host... An horse is a vain
thing for safety: neither shall he deliver any by his great strength"
(or in German: "*Einem Könige hilft nicht.seine große Macht...
Rosse helfen auch nicht, und ihre große Stärke errettet nicht*"). Of
this Harries had made,

Nicht Roß und Reisige
Sichern die steile Höh',
Wo Fürsten stehn.

(Nor horse nor mighty host
Cover the solemn height
Where princes stand.)

And since at the time Jacobin-baiting was in its prime, delicate
noses detected in David's words a smell of Revolution and Violence.
By the skin of his teeth the poor little candidate escaped being
locked up for his patriotism. His poem strikes us today as a per=
fectly competent but uninspired performance. Immortal fame and
glory are due him, however, for having been the first to juxtapose
the German words "*Wonne*" and "*ganz*" which millions of Ger=

man-speaking children have since conceived to be *"Wonnegans"* ("goose of bliss") in the firm belief that it was a respectful reference to some monarch's wife.

Meanwhile the text published in Denmark embarked on a career all its own. On December 17, 1793, a German adaptation appeared under the title of *"Berliner Volksgesang"* in the *Spener'sche Zeitung*. Its first stanza was

> *Heil dir im Siegerkranz,*
> *Herrscher des Vaterlands,*
> *Heil König dir!*
> *Fühl in des Thrones Glanz*
> *Die hohe Wonne ganz:*
> *Liebling des Volks zu sein.*
> *Heil, Herrscher dir!*

> (Hail thee in victor's crown,
> Thou rul'st the land we own!
> Hail thee, o King!
> Feel on thy splendid throne
> This joy supreme alone
> To be thy people's choice! —
> Hail, ruler, thee!)

Before long it became known that the letters "Sc" over which the poem had been printed stood for the name of a certain Dr. Balthasar Schuhmacher. When he was accused of having drawn somewhat too freely on the Danish version, he proceeded to write another for which concert singer Friedrich Franz Hurka — well known at the time not only for his voice but also as a composer of songs — was prevailed upon to furnish a new arrangement of the British melody. However, the song attained the status of a Prussian national anthem only through a dramatic occurrence, not unlike the happenings in the case of the Austrian anthem or — through the above-mentioned performances by Drs. Arne and Burney in 1745 — in that of the original "God Save the King." *Kapellmeister*

Bernhard Wessely (1768–1826) was looking for a "hit" to adorn the performance of Rambach's patriotic play, *The Great Elector of Rathenow*, and decided to use our song as an intermezzo. At the very first performance, on September 25, 1795, the public was enthusiastic. Shortly thereafter, when on October 7 King Frederick William attended a repeat performance of the play, his entrance was highlighted by the intonation of *"Heil dir im Siegerkranz."* Contemporary reports tell us that "the audience joined in with emotional warmth." From this moment on the British melody was the Prussian national anthem.

There had been similar attempts to introduce the anthem in Austria. As early as 1782 one August Niemann produced in honor of Joseph II an adaptation of the British original:

> *Heil! Kaiser Joseph, heil!*
> *Dir, Deutschlands Vater, heil!*
> *Dem Kaiser heil!*

> (Hail, Caesar Joseph, hail!
> Germany's Father, hail!
> Emperor, hail!)

From time to time it was actually sung in this version which — to be quite exact — has the honor to have been the earliest continental adaptation of the British anthem. However, since the publication of Haydn's anthem in 1797, the British melody disappeared again. It was luckier in German lands, and little by little it came to be sung in Bavaria, Saxony, Württemberg, Baden, Hesse, Mecklen= burg, and Schwerin with the most varied texts — all of them breathing the spirit of immutable devotion to the ruling prince. Its appearance in tiny Liechtenstein is not free from unintentional humor. Here the text ran:

> *Oberst am jungen Rhein*
> *Lehnet sich Liechtenstein,*
> *In Alpenhöh'n.*

Das liebe Vaterland
Hat Gottes weise Hand
Für uns erseh'n.

(Up on the youthful Rhine
Is leaning Liechtenstein
In Alpine heights.
This cherished fatherland
Gave us the Lord's wise hand,
Ours by rights.)

In Switzerland it appeared with the following words:

Rufst du, mein Vaterland?
Sieh uns mit Herz und Hand
All dir geweiht.
Heil dir, Helvetia,
Hast noch die Söhne ja,
Wie sie St. Jakob sah
Freudvoll zum Streit.

(Callest thou, fatherland?
See us, with heart and hand
All thine for life.
Helvetia, hail to thee,
All thy sons wish to be
As them Saint James did see,
Joyful in strife.)

This text was done in 1811 by Johann Rudolf Wyss, Jr. (1782 to 1830). There is also a French text by H. Roehrich with the first stanza:

O monts indépendants,
Répétez nos accents,
Nos libres chants!
A toi, patrie,
Suisse chérie,
Le sang, la vie
De tes enfants.

(Unconquered mountains strong,
Carry the call along
Of freedom's song!
To thee, o fatherland,
Beloved Switzerland,
Thy children's heart and hand
Ever belong.)

In the United States, Samuel F. Smith (1808—1895) was the author of a freedom-praising text to go with the British anthem. It was written in 1832 and attained general popularity especially in the North at the time of the Civil War. Today "My Country" is next to the "Star-Spangled Banner" the most frequently sung semi-official national anthem in America. It has found a place in the American Hymnal.

In Sweden the song is sung with the words, "Bevare Gud vår Kung" ("God save our King"), again in combination with other unofficial anthems. But all this does not by any means complete the list of foreign adaptations of Britain's royal anthem.

One naturally wonders about the reasons for the fabulous popularity of this melody. They must no doubt be looked for deep down in human psychology. The simplicity of the structure of the song is certainly again an essential factor. Being simple it gives the impression of something familiar, a characteristic which it shares with all popular "hits." There is, to begin with, the juxtaposition of two fundamental rhythms which together represent the galliard rhythm ♩♩♩.♪♩, while the "head motive" consists of a phrase with which every child is familiar and which moves about the central note G. It is an optimistic and very well-balanced phrase which expresses confidence but keeps aloof from exaggerated emotionalism. Beyond this we must not forget of course that the immense moral and political respect which England inspired during the eighteenth century may have been the most important cause for the unparalleled spread of the anthem.

There is nothing surprising in the fact that we encounter similar

melodies in all ages. The anthem just happens to belong to the
large group of everyman's melodies which are also the migrating
melodies *par excellence*. And here of course we touch the real
reason for its contested authorship. To be absolutely fair, we
would have to state that the tune simply has no composer. The
phrase was in the air. It was never really composed or — if one
prefers — it was recomposed all the time. Long before Carey we
find the following melody in a collection of songs, sonatas, and
fugues which was published in 1728 by Georg Philipp Telemann
(1681—1767) under the title of *Der Getreue Musikmeister (The
Faithful Music Teacher)*:

When Anton Dvořák came to America in 1892, it was this theme
which occurred to him for his cantata, *The American Flag*, — a
theme, by the way, which he expected most probably to serve
eventually as the American national anthem:

And when Kalakaua, the King of Hawaii, decided in the nineties
to compose a national anthem for his country, the theme he chose
was this:

It would indeed be easy to go on indefinitely with this enumera= tion of conscious and unconscious adaptations.[7]

"God save the King" has been the source of inspiration for major and minor works of several composers. The first in their ranks was Handel who used it in his *Occasional Oratorio*, a treat= ment of the distress of the British who at the time (1746) were threatened by Scottish rebels. Beethoven — the man who wrote in his diary, "I must show the British what a godsend they have in their 'God save the King'" — used the anthem (as well as "Rule Britannia") in his *Battle of Vittoria*. Carl Maria Weber must have overlooked the fact that the anthem is British when in 1818 he wrote his *Overture of Jubilation* on the occasion of the fiftieth anniversary of the accession to the throne of King Frederick Augustus I of Saxony. At the time of the overture's first performance, it was precisely the anthem — used as a climactic conclusion — which swept the audience off their feet in a frenzy of enthusiasm. They all heard in this song, which affected them so deeply, nothing but the Saxon royal anthem, and no one gave heed to the fact that it was of British origin.

Then there is a *Festival Prelude (Festpräludium)* by Paul Janssen, formerly professor at the Dresden Conservatory. It is a four-handed (and four-footed) organ piece and bears the inscription, "With the use of the Saxon Royal Anthem, God bless the King." Minor and major geniuses have adapted the anthem, have used and abused it, and some have raised it into the realm of great art. This is especially true in the case of Brahms and his "Song of Triumph."

It is safe to assert that the British anthem is the anthem of anthems.

It will be remembered that "God save the King" was performed in 1745 in two theaters in London. It was Thomas Augustine Arne who had arranged it for the orchestra which played it at the Drury Lane Theater. Five years earlier, this same Arne had composed the music for two masques, *The Judgment of Paris* by William Con= greve and *Alfred,* the authors of which were two Scotchmen, James Thomson and David Mallet, the latter being in the employ of Frederick, then Prince of Wales. One of these performances (on August 1) was staged in celebration of the anniversary of the accession in 1714 of George I, formerly Elector of Hanover. In a way it is surprising that the celebration which included the masque *Alfred* had been arranged upon orders given by Prince Frederick, for at the time his bitter quarrels with his father, George II, were in full swing. Now, George II — who knew as little English as his predecessor, George I — spent a great deal of his time — again like his predecessor — in his native city of Hanover, where he liked to arrange court festivals in perfect accordance with German taste. When Frederick heard of such an affair, he hastened to make ar= rangements for a typically English celebration at Cliffden. And of that a masque was considered an indispensable ingredient.

Specific details about this semi-opera *Alfred* will be found in an article by Eduard Rimbault Dibdin, "The Bi-Centennary of Rule Britannia," in the British periodical *Music and Letters* (1940). The historical background is the Danish invasion of Britain and its re= conquest by King Alfred. Numerous characters appear. At the be= ginning the shepherd Corin and his wife Emma discover a stranger who, it transpires, is none other than King Alfred. Then there is a hermit who takes the part of a wise and kindly mediator, and finally Alfred's wife, Eltruda. We find the pastoral scenes, which were a prerequisite of this type of work, presented for once with an heroic angle. The "Genius of Britain" appears and conjures up all the great rulers of the island empire from Edward III to Queen Elizabeth. In conclusion Emma sings a charming but entirely un= heroic song while the hermit contributes the famous ode, "Rule Britannia," which was destined to be sung by thousands and thousands of British patriots in days to come long after the rest of the masque was completely forgotten. The finale is the pro= phetic bard's exhortatory address to Alfred to gather Britain's strengths and chase the enemy from the land.

It is possible that Prince Frederick's reason for not entrusting the composition of the masque to the most likely candidate, that is, to Handel, was that he considered him unfit for the assignment on account of his German nationality. Perhaps it was an act of oppo= sition on the part of the Prince who — though born in Germany himself — resented his father's consciously German attitudes. At any rate, it seems that Handel did not take it amiss, for if he had, he certainly would not have worked the ode into his *Occasional Oratorio.*

In 1804, Beethoven not only published seven variations on the theme of "God save the King" but also another five on "Rule Britannia." And just as "God save the King" appears in his *Battle Symphony,* so "Rule Britannia" is used there in the guise of an "English March." It is placed opposite the "French March," that is, the march of "Marlborough," and both are played by separate groups of wind instruments. "The English march should not be played too fast," Beethoven notes, but what he means is obviously that throughout the "Attack" there should be a gradual and steady increase in speed.

Well, it is not Beethoven's best work in which he assigned so distinguished a role to the British national anthem. But "Rule Britannia" has made other inroads into the realm of real art. Thomas Attwood (1765—1838), the British composer, disciple and friend of Mozart, used it in his *Coronation Anthem,* and Sir Alex- ander Campbell Mackenzie (1847—1935) took it up in his over= ture, *Britannia.*

While "God save the King" is Britain's royal anthem, "Rule Britannia" is the anthem of the British Empire. "God save the King" is a prayer; "Rule Britannia" is a proud — one feels tempted to say, imperialistic — hymn of victory. Its style is Handelesque, triumphant, warlike, self-possessed. It is, characteristically, an inter-British product; the composer Arne was an Englishman, the poet James Thomson a Scotchman, and its first public interpreter, the singer Quin, was Irish.

Wagner was so deeply impressed by the tune that in 1837 he wrote an overture *Rule Britannia* which he offered later on to John Smart, director of the Philharmonic Society in London. It was turned down and came to be considered lost until it was rediscov= ered in 1904. An interesting detail, which has not so far been noted, is the fact that in one passage in *Tristan* Wagner harks back to this *Rule Britannia*. It is the passage where Isolde has Tristan ordered to appear before her whereupon Kurvenal — having re= jected the request transmitted by Isolde's servant, Brangaene — sings the song which relates Tristan's victory over Morold while Brangaene withdraws in anger:

> *Sein Haupt doch hängt im Irenland*
> *Als Zins gezahlt von Engelland,*
> *Hei! Unser Held Tristan,*
> *Wie der Zins zahlen kann!*

> (His head yet hangs in Ireland
> A tribute paid by Angleland.
> Ho! Our great Tristan,
> What tribute-paying man!)

In the last line Wagner cites a phrase from his overture, *Rule Britannia*, specifically the conclusion of the introductory *maestoso*, and as we listen more carefully, we find that it is the phrase which corresponds to the words, "sang this strain." Whoever com= pares Kurvenal's song with "Rule Britannia," cannot fail to note that Wagner was decidedly influenced by the British tune when he conceived Kurvenal's sarcastic outburst. As a matter of fact, Wagner's use of the Rule-Britannia motive stands here as a symbol of England's dominion — restricted in this context, it is true, to her relationship with Ireland.

Wagner had the greatest respect for the Rule-Britannia anthem. He expressed his view that the first eight measures were musically the most characteristically typical expression of the British race. It is hard to disagree with him. As British self-possession, trust in· victory, and pride coupled with religious emotions are expressed in Handel's music — with the result that this composer could be re= garded as the musical representative of the British Empire — so the same spirit is alive in Arne's melody. But of course, it is quite possible to apply Wagner's view to other anthems in their relation to the countries that created them. There are not many anthems which do not correspond somehow to the national characteristics of the people which they represent. That is why an analysis of the musical and psychological character of national anthems is inter= esting not only from the point of view of the historian of music but also from that of the student of ethnology.

AUSTRIA

The **Austrian** anthem, *"Gott erhalte . . ."* ("May God save . . ."),
enjoys the unique distinction of being the only national anthem
which has for its composer one of the great masters of music:
Joseph Haydn. While it is difficult to understand why Germany
should have had no real national anthem of its own, it certainly
seems natural that Austria, the country to which the world is in=
debted for the great classical composers, should also be — or at
least have been — in possession of the most beautiful national
anthem. It is the pearl among all anthems, and none other has been
examined nearly as often and nearly as thoroughly from a musical
point of view.

We must visualize the political situation at the time of its
genesis. Austria was passing through a grave political crisis. Na=
poleon's might was in the ascendency, and the arch enemy of the
Hapsburgs, France — now Jacobinic, revolutionary, and hence
dynamically expansive — was a threat to the very existence of
Austria. The waves of the French Revolution seemed to engulf all
Europe, and the Hapsburg throne shook ominously in its founda=
tions. If the new French ideas had penetrated the Austrian states
which the Hapsburgs had held in tutelage for centuries, the result
would have been a national and social emancipation both on the
part of the various peoples comprising the empire and also on the
part of the so-called lower classes of society. And signs pointing
in the direction of such a development were plentiful indeed. In
1796 and 1797, Napoleon had marched into Italy liquidating a
number of minor independent principalities. He defeated the
Austrians not only on Italian soil but also in Austria proper, that
is, in Tirol which was handed over to Napoleon's puppet state of

Bavaria. Austrian troops were fighting the French in the Rhineland too. Napoleon threatened the very capital, Vienna. He invaded Styria and put the Viennese court in a state of panic. The Austrian order was hit to the core.

This is the atmosphere which inspired Haydn when he wrote his *Kaiserlied*. The actual composition was completed during the first days of the year 1797, and we are told that not only the execution but the very idea that Austria should have a song like Britain's "God save the King" goes back to Haydn himself. He had been in England twice, first from 1790 to 1792 and then again from 1794 to 1795, and it seems obvious that he must have been impressed by the dignity and respect which the British anthem commanded in that country. Now, at a time when Austria was in dire straits, the creation of a national anthem seemed doubly in=dicated.

Haydn turned to his friend and patron, Baron van Swieten who was an influential Maecenas in the field of music and played an important part in the lives of both Mozart and Beethoven. Through Swieten the idea was passed on to the President of Lower Austria, Francis Count Saurau, who took it up immediately, for he was intelligent enough to understand how eminently suited it was to galvanize the patriotism of the Austrian population and conse=quently their will to fight and die for the fatherland. At the same time it is likely that Saurau wished to promote himself in the good graces of the ruler. At any rate, it is interesting to note how early the principles of mass psychology were practiced in times of war.

Saurau proceeded to commission a third-rate poet by the name of Lorenz Leopold Haschka to compose a suitable text for the anthem. The composer of course was to be Haydn, who after all had originated the idea — a fact, by the way, which did not prevent Saurau at a later time from claiming to be the father of the Austrian national anthem. In all fairness it must be conceded that he did promote Haydn's plan with all the means at his disposal.

Haschka, the author of the Austrian text, is not exactly a shining light in the annals of literature. He was born in Vienna, on Sep=

tember 9, 1749. His name is Czech and might be rendered in English as Quencher. Early in life he decided to take holy orders and entered the Society of Jesus. During the liberalistic era of Joseph II it became fashionable to display enlightened and free-thinking attitudes, and the poet jumped promptly out of the cloth and became a freemason. However, after the death of Joseph II a new era of reaction set in, and Haschka found it expedient to return to the Church and even to act as a secret police informer. His opportunism paid off. He was given a professorship for aesthet= ics at the Theresian Academy and subsequently became custodian of the Viennese University Library. He died, well-appointed and with all civic honors, in 1827 at the age of seventy-eight. His poems, which include an "Ode to Gluck," were not too well re= ceived, and Goethe saw fit to administer to him one of his pungent *Xenia*. However that be, this little pseudo-poet cannot be denied the distinction of being the author of one of the most famous national anthems, of having written the words for one of the most beautiful songs in the music of the world.

After Saurau had given his *imprimatur* on January 28, 1797, every effort was made to render the song as popular as possible. The first performance was scheduled for February 12, the birthday of Emperor Francis. Copies of the song were on sale in all music stores. The emperor's favorite theater, the *Burg,* had put on for the occasion the comic opera *Doctor und Apotheker* by Ditters= dorf, and the new song was to be sung by the entire audience before the curtain rose. For this purpose text and music were distributed to everyone present.

There are contemporary reports which tell us that while the anthem was being sung the emperor stood deeply moved in the rear of his box, and only when the ovations would not come to an end did he finally step forward in token of his gratitude. How well the propaganda machine functioned may be gathered from the fact that the very same night the performance of the song was also carried out in Graz, Prague, Leoben, Innsbruck, and even Trieste, which at the time was already threatened by Napoleon's advance.

In a single day the song was a folk song. Everybody talked about "*Gott erhalte*"; nobody asked who the composer might be. And perhaps this very anonymity may be taken to be Haydn's greatest success. Still, Haydn did receive a gold box adorned with the portrait of His Majesty. The letter which Haydn sent in reply to Saurau is typical in its modesty. "Excellency," he wrote. "Such a surprise and such grace, especially about the portrait of my kind monarch, I have never experienced in view of my modest talents. I thank your Excellency with all my heart and am ready to serve your Excellency at any time. Until 11 o'clock I shall submit the [printer's] proof. I am, in deep respect, your most submissive and obedient servant, Jos. Haydn."

Indeed, Haydn's melody inspired a wave of patriotic enthusiasm which in manner and kind remains unequaled in the annals of history. Not even the effects produced by the "*Marseillaise*" can be compared, for the enthusiasm which was released by the new French national anthem went hand in hand with the mighty psychological upsurge inherent in the Revolution as an historical fact. Austria's "*Gott erhalte*" was, however, a merely defensive anthem. Through it the intrinsically divergent peoples of Austria, held together by nothing but the ruling house of Hapsburg, were inspired by a common enthusiasm for the defense of state and dynasty. For more than a century, "*Gott erhalte*" proved its galvanizing force. Whenever its strains were heard, everyone stood at attention; all men removed their hats and caps; and a tremor of sublime reverence cast its spell over the multitudes. It was a religious song. It was a prayer. But it was a command as well. It was a symbol of the milennial tradition of the House of Hapsburg.

From a musical point of view, a great deal has been written about the song. Just as there have been attempts to deny the British the authorship of their national anthem, so Haydn too has been accused of plagiarism. In 1837 it was "discovered" that not Haydn but the Italian composer of operas, Nicola Antonio Zingarelli (1752—1837), was the real composer of the song. The facts of the matter are these: After its first publication, the Austrian anthem was naturally translated into the languages of all Austrian peoples. One of Haydn's most ardent admirers, who was also one of his biographers, Giuseppe Carpani, translated the anthem into Italian. It was this translation which Zingarelli used in one of his own compositions. The work in question found little favor, but it is hardly surprising that it came to be regarded — especially among Italians — as proof that the famous imperial anthem was really composed by an Italian. As a matter of fact, Anton Schmid, the biographer of Gluck, felt called upon to write an entire book in which he untertook to prove the authorship of Haydn in meticulous detail. And yet — however clear the authorship question would appear to be — time and again voices have been raised in favor of airing it anew.

There is, for instance, the Croatian folklorist Fr. Kuháč who was satisfied that he had demonstrated Haydn's Croatian descent and then proceeded to maintain that the composer had simply "taken" the tune from the Croatian folk song treasure. The arguments which he outlined in his book, *Josip Haydn: Hrvatské Národne Popievke* (Agram, 1880), were taken up by W. H. Hadow in his study, *A Croatian Composer* (London, 1897).

It may be of interest to take a look at the Croatian folk songs on which Kuháč and after him Hadow tried to base their theories. Kuháč quotes two such songs as alleged models of Haydn's anthem. The text of the first one begins, "*Stal se jesem rano jutro.*" Its melody, in a version from Marija Bistric, reads as follows:

Another version comes from the Mur Island:

It is easy to see that Kuháč was struck by the initial motive. But this is merely one of those ever-recurring tonal phrases which are rooted in the primeval law of the melodic up and down. In this case we have the ascending and descending tetrachord:

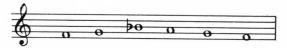

Thus Mary Magdalen sings according to a fourteenth-century manuscript in the Prague library with the words, *U-bi est spes me-a?*, the tune:

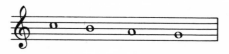

Similar tonal phrases can be traced by the dozen throughout the Middle Ages.

What has been said about the initial motive holds equally true for the descending diatonic fourth:

It is found a thousand times in folk song and art music. Haydn himself had used it previously both in his Mass in C Major and in the "*Sieben Worte des Erlösers am Kreuz*" ("Seven words of the Redeemer on the Cross"). There can be no doubt but what Haydn was familiar from his earliest youth with these phrases so generally encountered in folk and children's songs. But this does not mean at all that he borrowed them consciously. After all, Kuháč's Croa= tian folk songs are likewise based on an international children's-song pattern. A long time before Haydn, when Croatian folk songs were totally unknown in Europe, Reinhard Keiser, the gifted friend of Handel, had written as part of his opera *Circe* (1734) the following arietta with the text, "*Auf die Gesundheit aller Mädchen*" ("Here's to the health of every maiden"):

Is that possibly also a Croatian folk song? We know that most Croatian folk songs are in minor, not in major, and the Croatian folk song here under discussion may well have been a Northern immigrant from Austria unless it be the Haydn anthem which influenced it — and that is by no means unlikely.

After all, Mozart's arias, sung about 1787 by the street urchins in Prague, have had an entirely comparable influence on Czech folk songs. I have been able to show in my book, *Mozart in Bohemia*, that several Czech folk songs are directly based on Mozart melo= dies. Czech musicologists have demonstrated that the vast majority of the Czech folk songs which are sung today arose in the eighteenth century. And there is hardly any doubt that the same holds true for Croatian folk songs as well. At any rate, the theory of a Croatian Haydn and consequently its offspring, the theory of the Croatian origin of the Austrian national anthem, should be regarded as definitely and definitively discredited. I feel I should make this explicit statement because Hadow's book about Haydn, the Croatian composer, has many adherents in the Anglo-Saxon world.

The best discussion of Haydn's anthem is the one by Alfred Heuss in the first volume of *Zeitschrift für Musikwissenschaft.* Here, as elsewhere in his writings, Heuss develops the view that the composer of a strophic song does not simply follow the first strophe of his text but rather the one which makes the deepest impression on him. In the present case it is quite obvious that Haydn did not have the first strophe in mind when he composed the anthem, for the first strophe begins with the refrain, and the refrain throughout is musically marked by specially emphasized descending fourths which impart to the word *"Gott"* particular strength. In Heuss's opinion, Haydn thought of the last of Haschka's four strophes when he wrote the song. The fourth is distinguished from all the other strophes by its concrete contents. It would seem to have had special appeal for Haydn in human terms, for a line like, *"Er zerbrach der Knechtschaft Banden"* ("He cast off the bonds of serfdom"), has a certain affinity with Haydn's career which advanced from the status of a hired musician to that of an independent and autonomous artist. The most convincing argument in favor of this notion — that Haydn felt especially attracted by the fourth strophe — may be seen in the fact that music and text do not form a whole of comparable harmony in the case of any of the other three strophes. It should be noted, by the way, that Haydn did not write the tune in one fell swoop. A sketch preserved at the National Library of Vienna reveals that the second part ran as follows:

The popularity of Haydn's anthem led naturally to its use with other texts. As early as 1798, that is, one year after its first perform=

ance, it appeared as a freemasons' song in the collection, *Auswahl von Maurer Gesängen (Selection of Masons' Songs)*, edited by Boeheim. This is an interesting parallel to the Dutch freemasons' song which was written for the melody of "God save the King." — Then there was a text, "*Gott gieb unsern Waffen Siege, Friede dann dem Vaterland*" ("God grant our weapons triumph, peace then to the fatherland"). But it seems that the tune was not only suitable for patriotic, masonic, warlike, socially entertaining, and Heaven knows what other types of texts; it also revealed religious potentialities. In England as well as America it found its way into the hymnals of almost all denominations.

The following version is taken from Haydn's *Kaiser Quartett* (op. 76, nr. 3, in C major) where the master uses the song as the theme of this famous variations:

However beautiful the Austrian anthem may be, it did not escape interferences in the most deplorably bad taste. When Emperor Francis died on March 2, 1835, "*Gott erhalte*" was performed as part of one of the *Concerts spirituels* with a textual variant by J. F. Castelli in an arrangement for solo, chorus, and orchestra by Ign. von Seyfried. The text began, "*Gottes Ratschluß hat genom= men uns den guten Kaiser Franz*" ("In His wisdom God has taken Francis, kindest Emperor"), and the first two strophes appeared in minor. The third with the opening lines, "*Aber in den Kelch des Schmerzes mischt sich auch der Hoffnung Glück*" ("But into the cup of sorrow is infused the bliss of hope") was in major. Botstiber, who completed the great Haydn biography by C. F. Pohl, suggests that this feat of bad taste may have been perpetrated in compliance with a hint from the Austrian government.

Haschka's original text was bound to undergo a thorough revision. When Emperor Francis (*Kaiser Franz*) had died, the anthem was, as it were, a mourning survivor. Now the problem was to find another text, for Metternich, the famous statesman of Austria's reactionary period, was quite aware of the enormous psychological and patriotic virtues of the tune. However, the new emperor had a name in three syllables. He was called Ferdinand, and that made a simple adaptation quite impossible. The best solu= tion seemed to be a public contest, and when it was announced, fourteen poets participated, among them Franz Grillparzer, Karl Egon Ebert, Johann Gabriel Seidl, and Ignaz Franz Castelli.

Strangely enough, the text that finally found favor with Metter= nich was one which had few merits beyond the fact that it was recommended by Privy Councillor Jarncke, who was a native North German and had been professor at the University of Berlin. He had taken a certain interest in his compatriot, the actor, poet, and adventurer Carl von Holtei, and induced him to compose a text. It was a weak performance and aroused the ire of all Viennese men of letters who felt insulted when this North German upstart was allowed to rank above them. At all street corners pamphlets against the anthem were distributed and parodies appeared in great num=

bers. Among them there was one aimed at Privy Councillor Jarncke. It began, "*Auf dem Ballplatz sitzt ein Preuße*," which — since *Ball= platz* was the address of the Austrian Foreign Office — may be rendered as, "At the helm now sits a Prussian." There can hardly be a better illustration of the contrast between North Germans and Austrians than this ado about the Austrian anthem. The last lines of Holtei's version ran, "*Ja, den Kaiser Gott erhalte, / Unsern Kaiser Ferdinand*," where the word "*ja*" was drawn out into *ee-ah* so that it sounded like the German imitation of a braying donkey: "Hee-haw, may God save the Emperor, / Our Emperor Ferdinand."

Indeed, even the good-natured Viennese were ready to rebel in the days before 1848, but only when the issue at hand concerned a melody which they had taken to their hearts. — Finally the government had to give in. A new text was ordered and the poet Baron Joseph Christian von Zedlitz supplied one. It remained the official Austrian anthem until Ferdinand with his cognomen the Kind was forced to abdicate in 1848. When Emperor Francis Joseph ascended the throne, once again the time had come to look for another text. This time it was to be fashioned in such a way that the ruler's name would not appear in it. There had been more than enough trouble in this respect. From among the poets whom Prime Minister Baron von Bach invited to participate in the contest it was not Grillparzer with his beautiful but somehow too strongly intel= lectual verses but Johann Gabriel Seidl to whom the prize was given. Seidl's text was sung a million times till 1917.

When Emperor Francis Joseph died, a new text was asked for despite the lesson of past experiences. But the precipitous sequence of events·which swept the Hapsburgs off their throne resolved the problem by abolishing it.

It is only natural that Haydn's anthem, particularly in the begin= ning of its career, became a musical symbol of Austrian patriotism. During the time of the Napoleonic wars, a great wave of patriotism swept Austria and the anti-Napoleonic countries of Europe, leaving in its wake a large number of "battle pieces" and "tone poems" describing the various battles, campaigns, and victories.

I have in my possession a number of piano compositions which describe in great detail the return of Francis I to Vienna in 1809, the Battle of Leipzig on October 16 to 19, 1813, the jubilation over the news that the allies had taken Paris on March 31, 1814, and a number of similar events. These program compositions, which remind one of Beethoven's *Battle Symphony,* are filled with grenadier and cavalry marches, with trumpet calls and cannon shots, and in some cases, even the cries of the wounded.

So the *Sieger und Friedensfest der verbündeten Monarchen ge= feyert im Prater etc. am 18ten October, 1814, als am Jahrstage der Völkerschlacht bey Leipzig (Victory and Peace Celebration of the Allied Monarchs, conducted in the Prater etc. on October 18, 1814, as on the anniversary of the Battle of the Nations at Leipzig)* by Adalbert Gyrowetz contains, for example, a complete description of all phases of the occasion. It has, in addition to more joyful exuberations, a hymn of peace, and includes a dance to the music of a country organ-grinder. This dance is interrupted when the crowd catches sight of the Emperor, and characteristically enough, it is again Haydn's hymn which indicates his appearance.

Haydn's hymn was used in a similar manner by Anton Diabelli who produced another musical description of the same celebration, this time based on a poem by Kanne. Diabelli is probably better known as one of Beethoven's Viennese publishers and perhaps as the author of the theme of the *Diabelli Variations.*

Tobias Haslinger — another of Beethoven's publishers — was likewise among those who wrote and marketed numerous "battle pieces" as their contribution to this popular *genre.* His item, *Das neubeglückte Oesterreich oder Triumph des Wiedersehens bey Franz I. etc. (The Renewed Fortune of Austria, or the Triumph of the Return of Francis I),* depicts the event with fitting and charac= teristic candor, using again Haydn's hymn to symbolize the Emperor's entry.

For a while it looked as though Haydn's anthem were to live on as the official anthem of the Third Reich. It was sung with the well-known text, *"Deutschland, Deutschland über alles,"* which the nineteenth-century minstrel Hoffmann von Fallersleben (an itinerant reciter and promoter of his own poetic wares) had watered down from a beautiful poem by Walther von der Vogel=weide. Hoffmann wrote his modernized version of the Middle High German original on August 26, 1841, on the island of Heligoland which was then a British possession. During the Second Reich under William II, Hoffmann's text with Haydn's tune played the part of an unofficial national song and only through a decree issued by President Hindenburg on August 11, 1922, did it become the official anthem of the German Republic. During the Third Reich it had to share the honors of the German national anthem with the Horst Wessel song. But in course of time the latter was more and more often omitted from public celebrations, and thus it came to pass that Haydn's song appeared to be the sole anthem of Hit=ler's Germany.

Of the numerous instances where Haydn's anthem was intro=duced in other compositions, we must at least refer to the master's own *Kaiserquartett*. Haydn composed it in 1796. It is the third of six string quartets (op. 76) which were dedicated to Count Erdoedy. The first performance took place on September 28 as part of a court concert. In discussing it we must heed the view — expressed by several important musicologists like Alfred Heuss, Arnold Schering, and others — that most of Haydn's instrumental works (just like Beethoven's) were meant to express something quite specific, that they were in a sense instances of program music — though not exactly in the sense in which the term is used with reference to the later nineteenth century. Haydn himself has emphasized this point time and again as we know through the testimony of his friend and biographer Carpani.

The center of the *Kaiserquartett* is held by the variations on the theme of the national anthem. Heuss asserts that the other move=ments are likewise related to the anthem. The first movement —

characterized by a thematic concentration otherwise rare with Haydn — represents the Austrians' determination, the people's ardent desire to consolidate and resist the foreign aggressor. The second movement, which includes the anthem and four variations, expresses the people's devotion to the ruling house, and every variation — so this interpretation has it — alludes to one particular strophe of Haschka's poem. The minuet reflects the spirit of productive work of the rural population, while the final move= ment amounts to a noble and profoundly spiritualized portrayal of victory and liberation from a hateful foreign yoke. Here then — providing of course that the views of the scholars cited are cor= rect — we have the extraordinary case of a national anthem im= mortalized in a classical work of instrumental music which elevates it far above its functional realm.

♩♩ ♩♩ ♩♩ ♩♩ ♩♩ ♩♩ ♩♩ ♩♩ ♩♩ ♩♩ ♩♩ ♩♩ ♩♩ ♩♩ ♩♩ ♩♩ ♩♩ ♩♩

When the Austrian Republic was established after the close of World War I, the new rulers took it to be incumbent upon them to put an end to the old Haydn melody. It had too much of a Hapsburg flair about it. So in 1920 the Austrian composer Wilhelm Kienzl was approached, and he provided the music for Karl Renner's text, *"Deutsch-Oesterreich, du herrliches Land, wir lieben Dich"* ("O Austria, thou wonderful land, our love is thine"). We may skip this attempt without too great a loss. At any rate, the Austrians did not take to it. It was dethroned before long, and in 1929 Haydn's melody was re-instated with a text by Kernstock, *"Sei gesegnet ohne Ende / Heimaterde wunderhold"* ("Blessed be in time eternal / Homeland soil, so wondrous fair").

Yet this text did not survive for long either. It died away with the Hitler invasion which brought with it to Austria the text by Hoffmann von Fallersleben to serve with the traditional Haydn melody.

Austria was defeated but its national anthem had vanquished the victor.

And now for the final development which followed Hitler's collapse when Germany and Austria — to quote a satirical phrase coined by Erich Kästner — were once again "separated for ever and anon" after the brief interlude of their "eternal reunion."

The Haydn anthem, dearly beloved by all Austrians, seemed contaminated because it had been in Hitler's mouth. A new anthem was called for. Both melody and text were selected by a jury in a nation-wide contest held in 1946. The prize-winning poem — chosen from among two thousand entries — was a contribution by the Austrian poetess, Paula Preradovič. She was born in Vienna in 1887 from an old Croatian family and had published, before the time of her national triumph, five volumes of verse as well as several plays and novels. The text of her anthem breathes a spirit of quiet love of country rather than of political patriotism.

Land der Berge, Land am Strome,
Land der Äcker, Land der Dome,
Land der Hämmer, zukunftsreich!
Heimat bist du großer Söhne,
Volk, begnadet für das Schöne,
Vielgerühmtes Österreich.
Vielgerühmtes Österreich.

(Riverland of mountain ranges,
Land of churches, fertile granges,
Land of work, of prospects bright.
Great sons owe thee filial duty.
People graced with sense of beauty,
Austria, thou shining light.
Austria, thou shining light.)

The melody

is the last part of the *Little Freemason Cantata (Kleine Freimaurer-Kantate;* Koechel 623), the last composition completed by Mozart and written on November 15, 1791, less than a month before his death. The text of the Cantata was by Emanuel Schikaneder, the author of the libretto of the *Magic Flute.* It was written and composed for the inauguration in November, 1791, of the temple of the lodge *Zur neugekrönten Hoffnung (Newly Crowned Hope).* The last part of Mozart's composition became subsequently a very popular fraternal song. The text reads:

> *Laßt uns mit verschlungnen Händen*
> *Diese schöne Arbeit enden.*

> (Let us finish these fair labors,
> Hands united, helpful neighbors.)

The same tune was sung in students' organizations with the text, *"Brüder reicht die Hand zum Bunde"* ("Brothers, let our hands unite us"). Several scholars believe that the melody is not Mozart's since it is not found in the autograph proper but was added later on. They refuse to consider it a legitimate part of the cantata and there are some who feel certain that it was composed by Michael Haydn, a brother of Joseph Haydn. It is a fact that the *editio princeps* of the cantata, brought out by the printer Josef Hraschansky in 1792, does include the tune albeit only in an appendix. I for one feel inclined to consider the melody apocryphal and not by Mozart. There would seem to be a number of con= temporary Viennese musicians sharing my view as may be inferred from the bon mot currently in vogue in Vienna:

> *Wenn schon Mozart — dann Wolfgang!*
> *Wenn schon Haydn — dann Joseph!*

> (If it's Mozart — let's have Wolfgang!
> If it's Haydn — let's have Joseph!)

FRANCE

The "*Marseillaise*" is next to "God save the King" the most generally known of all national anthems. If the British anthem came to be in a sense the international prayer for the monarch, the French anthem became similarly the international "song of songs" of revolt. Yet — since here as elsewhere freakishness is the order of the day — the tune was by no means conceived as a tune of rebellion. Claude Joseph Rouget de Lisle (1760—1836), the man who composed it was no fanatic of democracy but a loyal subject of his king, a convinced partisan of the Bourbons. From April 1791 on, he was stationed at Strasbourg as a captain in the corps of engineers. He happened to be not only a good soldier but also a talented poet, singer, violinist, and composer and was by no means averse to letting his lights shine in congenial social gatherings. It was in particular at the home of Mayor Dietrich that the young officer distinguished himself among the literary and musical guests. In April, 1792, when Emperor Francis II and the Prussian King Frederick William II had concluded, at Pillnitz near Dresden, a pact designed to contain France and counteract the spread of her revolutionary ideas, she promptly proceeded to declare war upon the two Allied powers. The news reached Strasbourg on April 24, and at the Mayor's home Rouget de Lisle was urged to celebrate the occurrence in a patriotic poem. During the night of April 24/25, he wrote and composed the "*Chant de guerre pour l'armée du Rhin*" ("War Song of the Army of the Rhine"), and immediately the song was sung at one of Dietrich's gatherings. A lady friend of the house had produced a very amateurish piano accompaniment, for the poet and composer had noted down only the melody and a brief postlude for the violin. The song was published with the imprint of the firm of Th. J. Dannbach of Strasbourg and a dedication to Marshal Lukner, Commander-in-Chief of the Army of the Rhine.

The first Paris edition appeared a short while later with the imprint of the firm of Bignon. It contains the melody of the Strasbourg original and a piano arrangement full of typographical and other inaccuracies. In this as well as later editions, the name of the author is not mentioned. The song had already become a folk song. Its effect and success were unparalleled. Why it should have proved particularly inspiring at Marseilles is hard to say. At any rate, it was known there in June and was sung by one Mireur at a banquet given in connection with the dispatch of a battalion of volunteers to Paris. They were given printed copies of the text and sang the song all along their route. Three months after the "birth of the song," on July 3, they arrived in Paris, and when they joined the storming of the Tuileries on August 10, they sang and roared their favorite song in a frenzy of enthusiasm which imparted itself forthwith to the inflammable Paris mob. Because of the volunteers from Marseilles the song was called the "Marseilles March" and somewhat later simply the "*Marseillaise.*"

Little by little the author's name came to be known again, but the original significance of the song remained unremembered. The tyrants against whom Rouget de Lisle had meant to hurl his fiery tune, had been German princes, and the howling hordes of slaves he had in mind were German soldiers. Now the sense of it all was reinterpreted on the basis of the current revolutionary ideology.

On July 15, 1795, the "*Marseillaise*" was officially declared the national anthem of France, and henceforth it was sung at every state function, including every execution. There exist numerous contemporary reports which are all agreed as to the indescribable impression the song made wherever and whenever it was heard. The first strophes aroused an immense joy of battle which was mitigated by religious ardor in the final strophe, "*Amour sacré de la patrie.*" Everybody knelt down and rose again with the words,

"*Marchez, marchez,*" through which the warlike mood got again the upper hand.

Throughout the eighteenth and the first half of the nineteenth century, the Germans displayed a pronounced predilection for everything foreign, especially French, and hence they lost no time in translating the "*Marseillaise.*" The very year 1792 saw five different German versions. They are unimportant. But it may be of interest to refer in passing to the German "*Schlachtlied der Deutschen*" ("Battle Song of the Germans"), clearly intended as a counterpart to the French "War Song," "*Allons, enfants de la patrie...*" The "*Schlachtlied der Deutschen*" began:

> *Auf, rüstet euch, verbund'ne Heere*
> *Germaniens! Das Schwert zur Hand!*
> *Ein Volk, das Gott, Gesetz und Ehre*
> *Verhöhnt, droht unserm Vaterland.*
>
> (Up, gird yourself, united armies
> Of Germany! Take swords in hand.
> A people mocking God and honor
> And law attacks the fatherland.)

We see, a genuinely anti-French, anti-revolutionary text intended to be sung after the French tune! Similarly incongruous is the fact that the German poet Karl Alexander Herklots dedicated an anthem to Frederick William III of Prussia soon after his accession to the royal throne and wrote on its title page, "To be sung after the Marseilles anthem." This happened in the year 1798!

When Rouget de Lisle was confronted with the question as to whether he was willing to submit to the decisions of the National Assembly, his answer was a manly "No!" That was enough to make him lose honor and rank and to be put in prison. If Robes= pierre had not beaten him to it, the creator of the "*Marseillaise*" would have lost his head on the guillotine to the strains of his own music. He was spared such an ironic fate. In the fall of 1794 he reinlisted in the Army of the French Republic and advanced to the rank of commanding officer of a batallion. Already in 1796 he was definitively dismissed. His grateful country retired him without pay. With great difficulties he managed to make ends meet by doing odd jobs as a translator, newspaper correspondent, and music copyist. More than once did he find it expedient to retire early in order to save a meal; he was often obliged to call on the hospitality of the debtors' jail. There seemed to be within the confines of *la patrie* no job, no position — however humble — for the man who had written France's most popular song; a song which had fired millions with patriotic enthusiasm, which had won battles, to which the country owed no small part of its *gloire*. Late, very late indeed, in 1830, when during the July Revolution the *"Marseillaise"* once again had proved its power to inspire the masses, people suddenly remembered the old man who was now in his seventieth year. Louis Philippe granted him a pension of fifteen hundred francs — a paltry sum, yet enough to keep him from starving to death. When he died in 1836, large crowds of industrial workers escorted him bare-headed to his final resting place. To the strains of the *"Marseillaise"* his earthly remains were lowered into his grave. The interment took place at Choisy-le-Roy. It was only in 1915 that his body was exhumed and transferred to the *Dôme des Invalides* in Paris. From there it was eventually to be taken to the *Panthéon*.

The *"Marseillaise"* was a symbol of the Revolution, of liberty, equality, and brotherliness. Hence the fact that authorities in France as well as in Germany deemed it well-advised to outlaw the song at certain times. During the second Empire an attempt was made to replace the *"Marseillaise"* by another national anthem, *"Partons pour la Syrie"* ("March we will to Syria"), a piece written and composed by Hortense Eugénie de Beauharnais, the mother of Napoleon III. The words were rather inocuous; the melody was correspondingly pale. After the fall of Napoleon III, the nation returned promptly to the fighting tune of Rouget de Lisle. The following is the melody of the national anthem of the Second Empire:

When one compares the first edition of the *"Marseillaise"* with the version currently sung today, one is struck by a number of changes which the melody has undergone in the course of the one hundred and fifty years of its existence. Certain phrases — the very first for instance — were altered, intervals were worn down, and also the rhythm was affected in some places. "The people," or rather, constant and common use must be held responsible for these emendations in keeping with the style of the times. The text underwent fewer changes and variations did not begin to appear until the time of the Franco-Prussian war of 1870/71. It was then that the final lines of the refrain were replaced by the version, *"Marchons, marchons sur les bords du Rhin / pour battre les Prussiens"* ("Let's march, let's march down to the Rhine / to beat the Prussian line"); and when the French did not get the results they had hoped for, they began to sing, *"Marchons, ça ira, marchons, ça ira, / la république en France elle régnera"* ("Let's march — here we go — let's march — here we go. / Turn our France, turn France republican"). — There is also a supernumerary "stanza of the children" of unknown authorship which has variously been attributed to Marie-Joseph Chénier, the journalist Louis Du Bois, and the Abbé Antoine Pessonneaux. It begins, *"Nous entrerons dans la carrière"* ("We shall follow in their footsteps").

The *"Marseillaise"* shared the fate of "God save the King" and Haydn's Austrian anthem in that its composer was accused of plagiarism. Especially German periodicals were outspoken in their claim that the melody was taken from a mass by a certain *regens chori* Holtzmann. Even Tappert, an expert in matters of national anthems, insisted that the melody had been imported from Ger= many. Later on, it is true, he revised his verdict, but only when it had been ascertained that the composer Holtzmann (probably confused with Ignaz Holzbauer the famous composer of operas) was a legendary figure and that the mass (if it existed at all) was certainly of a more recent date than the French anthem. Still, it may not be devoid of interest to note that in Southwestern Germany an anonymous mass was found which dates back to about 1795 and whose "Credo" (*"Cre-do in u-num De-um, pa-trem omnipo-ten-tem"*) runs as follows:

As Istel has been able to show, the entire Holtzmann affair is a hoax perpetrated in 1861 by a certain J. B. Hamma (organist in Meersburg) through an article in the German family weekly, *Die Gartenlaube.* It was taken up by the reputed writer Alexander Moszkowski in 1915 in an article in the Berliner *Tageblatt,* but Hamma's arguments cannot withstand a thoroughly critical exam= ination. When he was urged to show the original of the "Credo," he explained that it had been sold to a rich American. The affair did cause a mighty commotion not only in Germany but also in France. The climax was reached in a lawsuit which involved the French historian of music, Fétis, who had attributed the song to the obscure composer Navoigille, and Rouget de Lisle's nephew, Amédée Rouget de Lisle. The latter won with flying colors.

The song spread rapidly all over the continent. In 1795 variations on it were published in Offenbach. The composer was Philipp Carl Hoffmann. It was reprinted in the music supplement to Possel's *Taschenbuch für die neueste Geschichte (Almanac of Current History*, Nuremberg, 1798). Direct and indirect traces of it are easily found in numerous so-called "country masses" — that is, masses which were composed by little country organists and specimens of which can even now be discovered in the attics of churches and parsonages throughout Germany and Austria. The anthem found its way also into the temple music of the Jews.

However, we must return once more to the question of its contested authorship. The 1934 edition of the German Brockhaus Encyclopedia does not hesitate to inform its readers that Rouget de Lisle composed the anthem in partial dependence on passages from Racine's tragedies, *Esther* and *Athalie,* and using note for note a melody from the introduction to the oratorio *Esther* by Jean-Baptiste Lucien Grison. Yet Tappert (1890) and after him Julien Tiersot (1892) had proved incontrovertibly that the "*Mar=seillaise*" was Rouget de Lisle's intellectual property both in terms of the text and also of the music. The fable that Grison was the composer has its origin in an essay by Arthur Loth who was an anti-revolutionary royalist. To gratify to his heart's content the urge to revile the poet of the revolution, Loth wrote an entire book contesting Rouget de Lisle's authorship, and that despite the failure on previous occasions of similar attempts in favor of Dalayrac, Grétry, Gossec, Méhul, Paer, Hermant, J. F. Reichardt, and many others. Also the violinist Alexandre Boucher and (in 1879) a certain Chevalier d'Hunn had been claimed to be the real authors.

It would take us too far afield — and add little or nothing to our story — to discuss here all the details involved in Rouget de Lisle's alleged plagiarism. The case of Grison, however, deserves a few additional remarks. This man, who was precentor and subsequently conductor at Saint-Omer, did write an oratorio *Esther*. In 1792 he began a series of patriotic concerts, and since he felt it his duty to flatter the republican powers, he simply plastered the "*Marseil=laise*" into his oratorio. Yet behold, the beginning of the plagiarized passage runs as follows:

Is not that rather a loan from Papageno, in Mozart's *Magic Flute*, who sings after this melody his famous "*Ein Mädchen oder Weibchen*" ("A lassie or a lady")? At a later time Grison followed Rouget's tune more closely. At any rate, as far as Rouget himself is concerned, he knew neither Grison nor his *Esther*.

In regard to Grétry we may note that this composer wrote in volume III of his memoirs, *Essais sur la musique* (1797): "The '*Marseillaise*' has been attributed to everyone who ever wrote an accompaniment for it. The author of this song, of both the words and the music, is the citizen Rouget de Lisle. He sent me his anthem '*Allons enfants de la patrie*' from Strasbourg, where he was stationed at the time, six months before it became known in Paris. In accordance with his wishes I had copies made and distributed." And yet, distinguished French historians and critics of music like Fétis and Castil Blaze were the ones who tried to deny Rouget de Lisle's authorship until Tiersot, Istel, and others helped the truth back on its feet.

The "*Marseillaise*," like so many national anthems, belongs to the large group of 'migrating melodies.' In Germany people sang (and still sing) a song taken from *Rinaldo Rinaldini*, the robber novel by Goethe's brother-in-law Vulpius. It runs, "*In des Waldes tiefen Gründen, / In den Höhlen tief versteckt...*" ("In the forest's yawning shadows, / Hidden deep in caves of rock ..."), and the burden relates how the robber lies in peaceful slumber, "*bis ihn seine Rosa weckt*" ("Till his Rosa wakens him"). Now, the tune

that goes with this refrain about the robber's passage from Mor=
pheus' into Rosa's arms proceeds as follows:

Böhme, in his *Volksthümliche Lieder der Deutschen* (*Popular
Songs of the Germans*; Leipzig, 1895), points out that the melody
to *Rinaldo Rinaldini* was in existence before 1800, and it is not
quite clear whether its last part was borrowed from the *Marseil=
laise* or had an earlier history of its own. Various portions of the
anthem are age-old, no-man's stuff that can be traced in hundreds
of melodies. So it is not surprising that the *"Marseillaise"* has
always been of particular interest to plagiarism-hounds. An ex=
ample is the passage, *"contre nous la tyrannie,"* which occurs in
an old German hymn, *"Der gold'nen Sonne Licht und Pracht"*
("The golden sun in light and pomp"):

And Mozart in his *Bandl Terzett* sings, *"Z'lebn in wah-rer
a-mi-ci-ti-a! und das schö-ne Ban-del ha-mer a"* ("To live in re-al
a-mi-ci-ti-a! and the pret-ty rib-bon we have too"), with the tune:

Almost a hundred years later, when Wagner in the first act of his music drama *Siegfried* had his hero sing: *"Aus dem Wald fort in die Welt ziehn, nimmer kehr' ich zurück..."* ("Leaving the woods for distant parts, never shall I return"), he used the age-old melodic phrase:

Rouget de Lisle's melody had a strange and remarkable career. One might say it shared the fate of its creator and of France. It was extolled to the skies and again banned and ostracized, precisely as its author was imprisoned and again praised as the "French Tyrtaeus." As previously suggested, in Vichy France the *"Marseillaise"* was *verboten* and sung only by the underground. Under the Fourth Republic it came to be *en vogue* again.

Even before World War I, it was defamed throughout Germany and Austria, not only because the melody was traditionally considered "revolutionary," but also because the Social Democratic Party used an adaptation of it as a rallying song for the laboring classes. The text of this "Workers' *Marseillaise*" with its timidly revolutionary sentiments was written by Jacob Audorf in 1864.

Numerous composers have used the *"Marseillaise"* in their works, thus imparting to them, as it were, a keenly characteristic profile. "The Two Grenadiers" by Heine is unthinkable as a song — especially in Schumann's version — without the *"Marseillaise."* The same holds true for Richard Wagner's version which — a strange coincidence, provided it is one — was written in 1840, the same year in which Schumann wrote his.

I remember an incident which occurred during the first World War when I served as an officer in the Austrian army. We had arranged a concert and I was to accompany the opera singer Rudolf Bandler who among other things had put Schumann's "The Two Grenadiers" on his program. After the concert we were called in by the commanding general. He explained to us that he had liked Schumann's song very much; but since it contained the national anthem of a country with which Austria was at war, he felt obliged — much as he hated it — to punish us by a two days' confinement to our rooms. He would, however — and he smiled as he said this — see to it that a piano be put in our quarters. He would visit us and have us repeat "The Two Grenadiers," just for himself alone.

Schumann, by the way, seems to have been extremely fond of the *"Marseillaise."* When he wrote in Vienna his *"Faschingsschwank aus Wien,"* he managed to smuggle the *"Marseillaise"* into it, but so skilfully that the censor of that pre-1848 era did not recognize it. Schumann also used the *"Marseillaise"* in his overture, *Hermann und Dorothea,* though only in order to characterize the historical background of Goethe's poem.

Among all the known compositions in which the *"Marseillaise"* has been employed, the most familiar example is doubtless Tchai= kovsky's overture *1812.* Here the French tune and the Russian na= tional melody, *"Bože, carja chrani,"* are presented in a sort of musical duel. Henry Litolff used the *"Marseillaise"* in his overture to Griepenkerl's tragedy *Robespierre.* Franz Liszt used it in his symphonic poem, *Héroide funèbre;* Arnold Mendelssohn in his opera, *Der Bärenhäuter (Lazy-Bones);* and Siegfried Ochs in his comic opera, *Im Namen des Gesetzes (In the Name of the Law)* But it occurs in numerous other works which we cannot begin to list, for it is the most forceful, the most energetic, and the most inspired of all national anthems.[8]

CENTRAL EUROPE

It is strange but true that both the most musical countries in the world, Germany and Italy, have produced no real national anthems. The explanation must no doubt be looked for in the German and Italian political past which reveals a good many parallels between conditions north and south of the Alps. In **Germany**'s case the national disruption, which has been for centuries the most striking trait of the country's history, would seem to have interfered with the formation and introduction of a general national anthem.

Until 1820, the German adaptation of "God Save the King" — *"Heil Dir im Siegerkranz"* ("Hail thee in victor's crown") — had no serious competitor. Occasionally Ernst Moritz Arndt's *"Was ist des Deutschen Vaterland?"* (What is the German's fatherland?"), written in 1813, was heard in either one of two musical settings. The first one was by Johannes Cotta who died in 1868 as a minister of the Gospel. He wrote it during his student days at Jena and thought of it primarily as a student's song. It was sung for the first time on June 12, 1815, at the Pine Tree Inn *(Gasthaus zur Tanne)* near Jena when the flags of the student fraternities were unveiled in a ceremony marking the founding of the liberal patriotic *Burschenschaft.* From then on it became one of the most popular patriotic songs. It must be considered one of the earliest Great-German manifestations for it proclaims the principle that all German tribes should be united under one rule. During the revolu= tionary epoch of 1848 it was sung at all rallies and meetings.

The melody with the words:

> *Was ist des Deutschen Vaterland?*
> *Ist's Preußenland, ist's Schwabenland?*
> *Ist's wo am Rhein die Rebe blüht?*
> *Ist's wo am Belt die Möwe zieht?*

> (What is the German's fatherland?
> The Prussians' land? The Swabians' land?
> Where on the Rhine the vineyards bloom?
> Where on the Belt the seagulls zoom?)

is the cue for the chorus to answer:

> *Nein, o nein, sein Vaterland muß größer sein!*

> (No, o no! His fatherland must greater be.)

And the first line of the last stanza reads:

> *Das ganze Deutschland muß es sein . . .*

> (It must be all of Germany . . .)

Cotta's tune has made thousands of hearts swell with patriotic fervor. It did however encounter a competitor in the form of Gustav Reichardt's setting. Reichardt (1797—1884) was a composer and singer and for a long time conductor of the Berlin *Liedertafel*. His melody

is musically superior but it never attained the popularity of Cotta's version.

Another pan-German anthem, especially in vogue at the time of the Franco-Prussian war of 1870, is the "Watch on the Rhine." It was written in 1840 by the young businessman Max Schnecken= burger, at a time when the French seemed to threaten the left bank of the Rhine. It did not, however, become generally known until after Karl Wilhelm, conductor in Krefeld, had given it a musical setting in 1854. It served the German cause during the war against the French so well that Empress Augusta decorated Karl Wilhelm in 1870 with the golden medal for art and science, and after the war, in 1871, the composer was granted a yearly stipend of 3000 marks. The text of the first stanza reads:

> *Es braust ein Ruf wie Donnerhall,*
> *Wie Schwertgeklirr und Wogenprall,*
> *Zum Rhein, zum Rhein, zum deutschen Rhein!*
> *Wer will des Stromes Hüter sein?*
> *Lieb Vaterland, kannst ruhig sein,*
> *Lieb Vaterland, kannst ruhig sein,*
> *Fest steht und treu die Wacht am Rhein,*
> *Fest steht und treu die Wacht am Rhein!*

> (Like bursting thunder rings a call,
> Like swords astir, waves' crashing fall,
> On to the Rhine, the German Rhine!
> Who to defend it falls in line?
> Dear Fatherland, rest and recline,
> Dear Fatherland, rest and recline:
> Loyal and firm they watch the Rhine,
> Loyal and firm they watch the Rhine!)

The tune which is generally known is as follows:

After 1870 the song was forbidden in Austria. It had become a propaganda song of the Great-German movement. When the struggle about the language rights of the Slavic minorities in Austria reached its various peaks of nationalistic fervor, the German-National faction in the Austrian Parliament would often use it as their song of protest and provocation; and it was truly a farcical manifestation of an otherwise serious problem when the Germans intoned their "Watch on the Rhine," the Czech's their *"Kde domov muj,"* the Poles their Dombrowski anthem — all with competitive passion — while a few modest Hapsburg die-hards tried to raise their timid voices to the strains of *"Gott erhalte."* It was the concert of Central European discord.

The several German national songs mentioned were not officially established anthems. In Prussia particularly the quest for a clear-cut national anthem had been going on for a long time. "Hail thee in victor's crown," sung innumerable times since 1795, was after all but an imported article. What was needed was a domestic product. And this led once again to one of those ironical situations in which history seems to take delight. The affair has to do with the composer Gasparo Luigi Pacifico Spontini (1774—1851) whose fame is founded on erverything but his having been the composer of the first German national anthem. In 1803 he had left his Italian home for Paris where he tried to get established as a composer of operas. His success was slow in coming. Finally, in 1807, his opera, *la Vestale*, came through with flying colors. Napoleon had offered a prize for the best opera and *la Vestale* was singled out for the honor. Thus Spontini came to be the foremost composer of the First Empire. Another Italian — after Lully and Cherubini — had been metamorphosed into a Frenchman. But this did not mark the end of Spontini's international career. The Prussian king, Frederick William III, had been in Paris in 1814 and there he had met the musician and taken a liking to him. The king wanted to attract

him to Berlin, and after prolonged negotiations Spontini was en=
gaged as General Director of Music and Conductor at the Royal
Prussian Opera. He drew a considerable salary and was merely
obligated to conduct his own operas and Mozart's *Don Giovanni.*
For everything else he had his sub-conductors.

He was the musical mogul of Berlin. There is an interesting story
which characterizes his enviable position well. When his opera
Olympia was staged in grand style in 1821, the head of the college
of censors issued a directive which warned all newspapers emphat=
ically not to find fault with Spontini's music in any way.

In course of time, however, the patriotic Berliners found Spon=
tini's position unbearable, and when on June 18, 1821, the opera
Freischütz was performed, its composer, Carl Maria von Weber,
was fêted like a three-quarter god. This meant a severe blow for
Spontini.

One of Spontini's first deeds in Berlin was the production "by
his majesty's most gracious commission" of a Prussian state
anthem to be known as "the Prussian People's Song." It was
written for soprano solo, solo quartet, chorus, and orchestra. Emil
Bohn in his book, *The National Anthems of the European Peoples,*
has characterized it succinctly as "proud, forceful, energetic, and
most effective but in no sense folklike." The text was a creation
of Joseph Friedrich Leopold Duncker, Cabinet Secretary to Freder=
ick William III. It is deplorable and most assuredly one of the
worst of its kind in German or any other language.

> *Wo ist das Volk, das kühn von Tat*
> *Der Tyrannei den Kopf zertrat?*
> *Groß, unbezwungen steht es da,*
> *Es ist dein Volk, Borussia.*

It is not altogether unfair to translate it thus:

> Where is the people, proud in fact,
> Through which the tyrant's head was cracked?
> Great, undefeated, there it stands,
> The people of Borussia's lands.

I must confess that I find the tune extremely synthetic and some=
how in keeping with the heroic style of the opera. What is a trill
doing in a popular anthem?

Yet Spontini's anthem did hang on in Prussia for more than
twenty years. In course of time, it is true, Spontini became the
best-hated resident of Berlin. On April 2, 1841, when he was about
to open a performance of *Don Giovanni,* he was literally hissed
out of the theater. That settled the fate of his Prussian anthem too.
But it came back to life about thirty years later. When the German
Empire was established in 1871, it was dug up again, and in the
month of August it was performed at the Royal Opera House in
Berlin. The soprano solo was sung — by the tenor Woworski. The
applause was enormous. The various text phrases which alluded
to Prussia had been altered. Wherever there had been a king, an
emperor was put in his stead, and *Borussia* had to make way for
Germania.

Now the Germans, finally united, had a national anthem of their
own. But it still was the work of a foreigner ... The unrelenting
quest for a truly German anthem singled out the poem, "I am a
Prussian," written by Bernhard Thiersch (1794–1855). But the
tune with which it was sung could not really pass muster. It was
French and belonged to the popular ballad, *„Brûlant d'amour et
partant pour la guerre"* ("Aflame with love and moving out to
battle"). There where other tunes which went with the poem: one
by Julius Schneider (1822), another by Wilhelm Greulich (1833),
and finally an adaptation of a chorus in Meyerbeer's opera, *Il Cro=
ciato in Egitto.*

But it was a tune composed by August Heinrich Neithardt (1793 to 1861) which finally assured the song its perennial appeal. Neit= hardt had taken part in the wars of liberation against Napoleon as an hoboist of the Prussian battalion of guards and spent his later years as a choir conductor in Berlin. When the adoption of new municipal by-laws for the city of Berlin served as the occasion for a great celebration with musical offerings on November 19, 1834, the opera singer Zschiesche, whose gigantic basso extended to the highest ranges of a baritone, approached Neithardt with the re= quest to produce for him a striking bravura piece. Neithardt picked out the poem, "I am a Prussian," and composed a new tune for it. It is not exactly folklike. It actually had coloratura passages in it. But it was striking and hard to get out of one's ears. To give Zschie= sche a chance to display his gorgeous voice in all its grandeur, Neithardt provided an accompaniment of hummed voices ("con bocca chiusa"). The tune found favor and became generally known, especially when Golde in 1842 used it together with "Hail thee in victor's crown" in his "119th Infantry March."

> Ich bin ein Preuße, kennt ihr meine Farben?
> Die Fahne schwebt mir weiß und schwarz voran.
> Daß für die Freiheit meine Väter starben,
> Das deuten, merkt es, meine Farben an.
> Nie werd ich bang verzagen.
> Wie jene will ich's wagen!
> Sei's trüber Tag, sei's heitrer Sonnenschein,
> Ich bin ein Preuße, will ein Preuße sein!
> Alt Preußenland, alt Preußenland,
> Mein Vaterland, — es lebe hoch! Hurra!

(I am a Prussian. Do you know my banner?
Its colors lead with black and white the way.
To die for freedom was my fathers' manner.
That, you must note, my banner does convey.
Ne'er shall I be despairing.
Like them I will be daring.

Be dark the day, be it of sunshine bright,
I am a Prussian, that is my delight.
Old Prussia mine, old Prussia mine,
My fatherland, — long may it live! Hurrah!)

After the reunion of the German states in 1871, "*Heil dir im Siegerkranz*" ("Hail thee in victor's crown") came to the fore again as the recognized German anthem. We have discussed this song in its proper place as an adaptation of "God save the king." Now the passage, "*Heil, Herrscher Dir*" ("Hail ruler thee") was brought up to date as "*Heil Kaiser Dir*" ("Hail Emperor thee").

In addition there was the tune of Haydn's "*Gott erhalte*," sung with the text of "*Deutschland, Deutschland, über alles*" which we have likewise discussed in its proper context as a variation of the Austrian anthem. When in 1933 the National Socialists took over in Germany, the "*Deutschlandlied*" (i.e., "*Deutschland, Deutsch= land über alles*") found a competitor in the party song known as the "*Horst-Wessel-Lied*."

Horst Wessel — born October 9, 1907, died February 23, 1930 — was the son of a pastor and joined the Nazi Party in 1926 in Berlin where he was matriculated at the university. In his endeavor to win over members of the Berlin proletariat for the Nazi cause he became the leader of the 34th SA (or storm troop) in the industrial suburb of Friedrichshain. In order to be near his men at all times, he moved to the district of his unit, gave up his work at the uni= versity, and earned his living as a chauffeur and dispatcher for the Berlin subway. There are persistent rumors that his relations with women of doubtful reputation were made to replenish his resources

with slight regard for "bourgeois" respectability. He pressed a re=
lentless private war against the Communists. In a street brawl he
was wounded and died at the Friedrichshain hospital from the
resulting blood poisoning. But Horst Wessel was also a "poet."
He wrote and composed the ill-famed song which starts

> *Die Fahne hoch, die Reihen dicht geschlossen,*
> *SA marschiert mit ruhig festem Schritt ...*

> (Lift up the flag, press close the rows of marchers,
> SA moves on with quiet, virile gait ...)

The text was often varied and the different versions would seem
to have been highly expressive of the sentiments of those for whom
the Horst Wessel Song was a sacred canticle. The best-known
textual deviation is the refrain, "When Jewish blood drips off
your knife, / The going is twice as smooth." The tune runs as
follows:

I recall having heard it (or fragments of it) in my early childhood
when people sang those primitive ballads of banditry as for in=
stance the story of Princess Kunigund whom her lover Edward
seduces and kills only to have her haunt his nights as a ghost.
Texts of this brand were sung with the tune later dignified as the
Nazi Party Anthem in dingy harbor pubs in Hamburg, and we are
told that that is where Horst Wessel picked it up. Its general pat=
tern is found in the street song:

> *Wenn grün die Eichen stehen auf den Fluren*
> *Und alles freuet sich der schönen Zeit,*

87

Muß Wilhelm fort in fremde Länder reisen,
Muß Wilhelm fort, fort, fort muß er von hier.

(When green the oaks are standing in the pasture
And all take pleasure in the season fair,
Then William must depart for foreign countries,
Must part with us, then William must depart.)

The Horst Wessel tune is merely a variant of the vulgar street ballad:

After the end of the Third Reich, both the Germanys emerging from the tension of East and West gave heed to the clamor for a new song of courage and national faith in the future of the father= land. It is one of the ironies of history that so far all efforts in this direction have proved abortive in Western Germany while East Germany or, as it is officially called, the German Democratic Re= public seems to have succeeded more than reasonably well.

The transformation of the East German people's council into a provisional people's Chamber on October 7, 1949, marked the establishment of the German Democratic Republic and was the occasion for the creation of a new national anthem. Both the poet, Johannes R. Becher, and the composer, Hanns Eisler, were veteran Communists of recognized achievements in their respective arts. The first stanza is poetically the only noteworthy one:

Auferstanden aus Ruinen
Und der Zukunft zugewandt,
Laß uns dir zum Guten dienen,
Deutschland, einig Vaterland.

Alte Not gilt es zu zwingen,
Und wir zwingen sie vereint,·
Denn es muß uns doch gelingen,
Daß die Sonne schön wie nie
Über Deutschland scheint.

(Out of ruins, thou, reviving
To forebuild thy future free,
For thy weal we shall be striving,
Thou, united Germany.
Ancient ills are to be righted.
Lo then! Righted they shall be,
And we reach the goal united
When the sun as never fair
Shines on Germany.)

Eisler's music, which follows the first stanza, reflects perfectly the "peaceful militancy" of the words. In keeping with them it is free from that languid sentimentality with which the new anthems of some "reformed" nations have replaced the imperialistic spirit of their old patriotic songs. The rhythm of the music corresponding to the first four lines is marked by an almost monotonously solemn sequence of quarter notes. A more varied rhythm for the next four lines mirrors the text's virile determination to build a prosperous future for the fatherland. The final line, "Shines on Germany," is repeated with the first two syllables corresponding once to two eighths and then to two quarter notes which device imparts to the conclusion of the song a certain hymnic finality.

Despite its undoubted merits this music tends to show on the whole that Eisler was very anxious to please both his German and Russian superiors. When one compares Eisler's ultramodern style in his "profane" works with this more than conventional anthem, the conclusion imposes itself that he must have tried to follow the rules of the "Central Art Committee" in order to escape the fate which befell many another individualistic pioneer in the realm of the arts in Communist lands. As a result, Eisler's anthem lacks both the immediate appeal of a folklike melody and the solemnity which springs from deep sincerity.

The Kingdom of the **Netherlands** has two equally current anthems of which the one, *"Wilhelmus van Nassouwe,"*

may be termed the royal anthem while the other, *"Wien Neer= landsch bloed,"* is rather a people's song. The two stand side by side, not unlike Britain's "God save the King" and "Rule Britannia."

"Wilhelmus van Nassouwe" is the oldest of all national anthems. It stems from the era of Dutch heroism, of the Dutch people's struggle against Spanish oppressors for freedom in politics and religion and is a folk song in the truest sense of the term.

As is generally known, the Dutch nobles, who worked in the sixteenth century, during the reign of Philip II, for the Nether= land's emancipation from Spanish rule, were called *gueux* or beggars. The appellation is said to have been coined by Count Barlaymont, president of the Council of Finances, while talking to Margaret of Parma about the Flemish nobles who were no= toriously in debt and had submitted, in 1566, a petition to King Philip. Very soon the term *gueux* was turned into a name of honor and a designation of party. It is in the ranks of these *gueux* that the song, or more specifically the ballad, of Wilhelmus was origi=

nated. It is found in their song book which was printed in 1581 under the title of *Nieu Geusen Lieden Boecken*. The oldest edition extant of melody and text together, is that contained in Adrianus Valerius' *Nederlandtsche-Gedenck-Clanck Tot Harlem* of 1626. But the tune was known in Germany about 1600. In 1603, the German composer Melchior Franck (ca. 1573–1639), a native of Coburg, included it in his *Opusculum Etlicher Newer und alter Reuterliedlein* in an arrangement for four voices adorned with a host of figures and melismata. A High German version had been printed in 1582 in the song book of Ambras.

We must take a look at the political situation in the Lowlands at that time. It was the unlucky year 1568. William (the Silent) of Orange had undertaken an unsuccessful expedition to the Lowlands. His brother, Count Adolphus of Nassau had fallen at Heilig= erlen in Frisia. The general mood was extremely depressed. Alva, the inexorable servant of King Philip's will, was biding his time in a fortified camp, waiting for the rebels to attack in order to annihilate them. Such was the state of things when the ballad of "Wilhelmus" was created, alledgedly by Philip Marnix of St. Alde= gonde, the friend and faithful supporter of William.

There are fifteen stanzas in all, composed as though spoken by William himself and beginning with the letters W-I-L-L-E-M V-A-N N-A-S-S-O-V. The general tenor is not one of confidence in victory but rather of resignation and at best of hope for comfort and redress in the life hereafter. The first stanza reads:

> *Wilhelmus van Nassouwe*
> *Ben ick van Duytschen bloet,*
> *Den Vaderlandt ghetrouwe*
> *Blijf ick tot in den doet:*
> *Een Prince van Oraengien*
> *Ben ick vry onverveert,*
> *Den Coning van Hispaengien*
> *Heb ick altijt gheëert.*

(My name is William of Nassau.
I am of Dutch descent,
True to the land of my fathers
Until my life is spent.
A prince I am of Orange,
A free man without fear.
Of Spain the King and ruler
I honor and revere.)

This is indeed an international song in more than one respect. Not only is the Dutch patriot William a German prince who respects the Spanish monarch, but also the tune of the song is in no sense regional. It is a migrating melody if ever there was one and must have been taken from some old-established song. In the song book of Ambras we find the notation, *"Im Thon wie der Graf zu Rom"* ("Same tune as the Count of Rome"). But the song of the Count of Rome, according to the same source, should in turn be sung after the melody of "Brother Vitus" which, however, has little in common with the tune as it came to be accepted later on. There are other editions which indicate the song should be sung after the melody of "Chartres" and again of "Charles." In one way or another it is most certainly a French song. Some experts who have taken up the question of its origin express the view that it was an old French hunters' song and there is nothing to disprove such a theory.

We find it as a Huguenot's song and can trace it in Germany from where it went on to Poland. There it was sung as a satire against the Polish King Henry III who had fled to France. In Switzerland the national song, *"Wilhelm bin ich, der Telle"* ("Tell they call me, and William") was sung after the same melody. In 1580 German soldiers sang the tune in Portugal, and in the seven= teenth century it was sung in France as a huntsman's song begin= ning, *"Pour aller à la chasse"* ("A-hunting we shall go").

From France the famous Bohemian Count Franz Anton Sporck, took it with him to Bohemia where it was sung by the hunters

on his estates under the name of *"Bon Repos* Aria" or also "Huber=
tus Aria." It is repeatedly referred to in the numerous secular and
religious writings of the militant count who allowed himself to be
drawn into an argument with the Jesuits. He seems to have been
very fond of it, so much so that he actually had it used with liturgi=
cal texts. In the little volume, *Christliche Kinderlehr (Christian
Children's Primer)*, which he had printed in 1721, he included an
engraving with a "Magnificat" after the old Wilhelmus tune in
this version:

Through Sporck the tune got into the works of Johann Sebastian
Bach. We may assume that the two men had met at Karlsbad. And
now the composer paid the Bohemian nobleman his respects first
by sending him the "Sanctus" from his great Mass in B minor and
then by using the count's favorite melody in his *Peasant's Cantata*
for the passage, *"Es nehme 10,000 Dukaten der Kammerherr alle
Tag ein"* ("A taking of ten thousand ducats the Chamberlain count
every day").

The tune has survived in Bohemia up to modern times. One of
the favorite songs of the German students at Prague was till quite
recently *"Nach Süden nun sich wenden / Die Vöglein allzumal"*
("To southern climes are turning / The birds from everywhere").
The beautiful text is by the German romanticist, Baron Joseph von
Eichendorff. It is generally known as the "Prague Student Song,"
and the tune was again that of "Wilhelmus."

Mozart too felt attracted by the tune from childhood on. A faith= ful friend of the family, court trumpeter Schachtner, is the authority for the story that Wolfgang had composed a tune when he was five years old. Every night, before going to bed, he insisted on singing it. His father had to stand him up on a chair and join in. During the performance little Wolfgang would kiss the tip of his father's nose. This nightly ritual was kept up till the boy was ten years old. But the tune which he had "composed" proved to be none other than that of *"Wilhelmus."* We have the evidence in Schachtner's quotation:

When Mozart was ten, his great trip took him to the Hague, and there he composed a sort of *quodlibet* — now it would be called a potpourri — under the title of *Galimathias Musicum.* The tune of *"Wilhelmus"* plays an important part in it, for — as Mozart himself put it — "in Holland everybody sings, whistles, and hums it." He also composed "Seven Variations on William of Nassau" (Köchel 25) with the following theme:

Time and again the tune must have been in Mozart's mind, for it is no rare occurrence that melodic ideas of his show the influence of the "Nassau Song," as holds true for instance for a theme in his "Violin Concerto in G Major" (Köchel 218) which he referred to as a "Strasbourg Dance."

The second anthem of the Low Countries appeared during the political upheaval in Belgium in 1830. After the fall of Napoleon, by virtue of both the Treaty of London of May 19, 1815, and the final protocol of the Congress of Vienna of June 9, 1815, Holland and Belgium were merged in one kingdom under the rule of Wil= liam I. Together the two countries entered upon an era of economic prosperity which, however, could not smooth over the national divergences. They assumed such proportions that after the victori= ous July Revolution in Paris, French influence sufficed to instigate a popular rebellion in Brussels on August 25, 1830. The attempt of Dutch troops to take Brussels was repulsed whereupon a National Assembly deposed the House of Orange. On June 4, 1831, the British candidate, Leopold I (of the House of Saxe-Coburg-Saalfield), was elected king.

The tide of nationalism was running high both in Holland and Belgium, and thus the new Dutch anthem and that of Belgium came to be written at about the same time. The Dutch text begins, *"Wien Neerlandsch bloed in d'adren vloeit"* ("Who Netherlandish blood in his veins feels throb"). It is the work of the Dutch poet, Hendrik Tollens (1780—1856). The music on the other hand was done by the German Johann Wilhelm Wilms (1772—1847), a native of Schwarzburg-Sondershausen, who had been living at Elberfeld until 1791 after which he resided in Amsterdam up to the time of his death. It is not a bad tune musically speaking. The middle part has something in common with "The Watch on the Rhine." What is missing is the characteristic dignity of the old "Wilhelmus Song," and so it is not surprising that the new anthem — now the official one — could not supersede its predecessor completely.

95

The **Belgian** anthem — as previously noted — owes its existence to the same Belgian-Dutch difficulties. Under the impression of the events of 1830, the French comedian and poet Hippolyte Louis Alexandre Dechet — more generally known by his pseudonym Jenneval — had come from Paris to fight with the Belgian patriots. He was killed in action near Lierre but not before he had written the first two versions of "*la Brabançonne,*" the song of Brabant. The first was sung on September 12, 1830, at the *Théâtre de la Monnaire* in Brussels, that is, at a time when Belgium was still part of the Kingdom of The Netherlands under the rule of the House of Orange. It pledged loyalty to the King provided it be allowed to ripen as a fruit on the tree of liberty. The second version, writ= ten during the street fighting in which Belgium won its independence, kept the theme of the tree of liberty but now no Orange could be tolerated on it. The first stanza of this second version reads:

Qui l'aurait cru? — de l'arbitraire
Consacrant les affreux projets
Sur nous, de l'airain militaire,
Un prince a lancé les boulets.
C'en est fait! Oui, Belges, tout change,
Avec Nassau plus d'indigne traité!
La mitraille a brisé l'Orange
Sur l'arbre de la Liberté.

(Can it be true? — To suit his craving
And satisfy his heinous lust
A princeling trains on us his cannon
Which death-imparting steel do thrust.
So it is! Belgians, all is altered:
With Nassau no more shameful pact!
The muzzles of our guns are blazing.
Off freedom's tree Orange is hacked.)

Such was the mood in the heat of the moment. Later on things got cooled off and people were eager again to establish good-neighborly relations. So in 1860, the famous liberal statesman

Charles Rogier (to whom Belgium is indebted for its public-school system) wrote a completely new text which omitted all allusions to Holland and its royal house but dealt instead exclusively with the glory of Belgium, reiterating in the last line of every stanza, *"Le Roi, la loi, la liberté"* ("For King and Law and Liberty").

The melody which had been composed by the singer François van Campenhout (1779–1848) was retained and in this form the anthem attained official recognition.

The melody has often been severely criticized. Some parts of it were influenced by contemporary popular hits. One may find traces in it of the song, in vogue at the time, *"Aux temps heureux de la chevalerie"* ("In lucky ages that knew chivalry"), or of the march in Rossini's *Tancred*. But on the whole *"la Branbançonne"* does prove its mettle as a fiery and inspiring tune. It has done so a thousand times and may be compared with the *"Marseillaise"* in more than one respect.

We have noted in connection with the British anthem that the **Swiss** sing *"Rufst du, mein Vaterland"* ("Callest thou, father=land") with the tune of "God save the King." More recently the "Swiss Psalm" with words by L. Widmer and put to music in 1841 by Father Zwyssig (1808–1854) is often heard.

> *Trittst im Morgenrot daher,*
> *Seh' ich dich im Strahlenmeer. ...*

> (Through the dawn's red light you go;
> I see thee in radiant flow. ...)

The **Latvian** national anthem is among those which Czarist
Russia saw fit to tolerate. Both text and music are by Karlis Bau=
manis or Karl Bauman, a teacher who was born in Livonia in 1835
and died there in 1904. The song was originally written as an entry
for the first Latvian singing festival at Riga on June 27 to 29, 1873,
but very soon its spontaneous popularity earned for it the status
of a national anthem. Under the Czars it was generally sung right
after the Russian anthem. When its strains were heard, everybody
arose and joined in, the men with bared heads.

Musically it is characterized by a sequence-like repetition of the
initial motive which resembles the German folk song *"Wenn ich
ein Vöglein wär"* ("If like a bird I were") and — more distantly —
the British Royal anthem. The second part sounds somewhat
amateurish and hard-pressed.

Dievs, svētī Latviju,
Mūs' dārgo tēviju,
Svētī jel Latviju,
Ak svētī jel to!
Kur latvju meitas zied,
Kur latvju dēli dzied,
Laid mums tur laimē diet,
Mūs' Latvijā.

(God bless the Latvian land,
Our dear fatherland,
Bless our Latvian land,
Bless it, o Lord!
Where Latvia's daughters beam,
Her sons forever dream
Her glory to redeem,
Our Latvia.)

The **Finnish** national anthem, *"Maamme"* ("Our Land"), was sung for the first time at a students' gathering on May 13, 1848. The text, first published the previous year, was by Finland's national poet, Johan Ludvig Runeberg (1804–1877), all of whose works — including the anthem — were first written in Swedish and subsequently translated into Finnish by the poets Paavo Kajander and Otto Manninen. The first stanza in Swedish and Finnish reads as follows:

Vårt land, vårt land, vårt fosterland!
Ljud högt, o dyra ord!
Ej lyfts en höjd mot himlens rand,
Ej sänks en dal, ej sköljs en strand,
Mer älskad än vår bygd i nord,
Än våra fäders jord.

Oi maamme, Suomi, synnyinmaa!
Soi sana, kultainen!
Ei laaksoa, ei kukkulaa,
Ei vettä, rantaa rakkaampaa,
Kuin kotimaa tää pohjoinen,
Maa kallis isien.

(O land of ours, fatherland!
Ring forth, thou precious word!
No skyward tow'ring mountain grand,
No sloping vale, no sweeping strand

This heart like our home has stirred,
Our fathers' home up north.)

The Finnish national anthem is one of the few whose texts were written by poets of distinction and hence display poetic merits worth commenting upon. The melody is likewise considerably more than an amateur's lucky hit. It is the work of the Finnish violinist and composer of operas and songs, Fredrik Pacius, who was born in Hamburg, Germany, on March 19, 1809, but lived most of his life at Helsinki where he died on January 9, 1891. He became the founder of the Finnish national school of music (1852) and is considered the father of Finnish opera. His *Kung Karls Jakt (The Hunt of King Charles)* after a libretto by Z. Topelius was the first Finnish opera and was received at Helsinki with great enthu=siasm. Many of his songs have proved so popular that they must now be classed as true Finnish folk songs. His anthem — without shift of key — is simple, forceful, and melodious. It has a certain distinctive boldness which makes it sound angular and massive.

Another national song, *"Herää Suomi,"* by Emil Genetz has not been able to supersede the Pacius anthem which begins as follows:

The **Estonian** anthem, *"Mu isamaa"* ("My Country") is an adaptation of Finland's *"Maamme."* Pacius' tune was kept intact while Runeberg's Swedish text was followed closely only in the first stanza. *"Mu isamaa"* is the work of Johann Woldemar Jann=sen (1819–1890) and was sung publicly for the first time at the first Estonian National Singing Festival in Tartu on July 1, 1869. From 1917/18 on the song has had the standing of a national anthem.

The **Lithuanian** anthem, *"Lietuva, tēvyne mūsu"* ("Lithuania, my country"), was written and composed by Vincas Kudirka (1858–1899). It first appeared in print in 1896 and has been the official national anthem since 1918. The tune was inspired by a religious melody sung by a group of pilgrims before the Shrine of the Blessed Virgin at the Eastern Gate in Vilna. In its opening bars it is not altogether different from the German folk song, *"Stimmt an mit hellem hohem Klang"* ("Strike up in joyous solemn song") by A. Methfessel (1818).

Although **Sweden** and Norway formed a single kingdom for a long period of time, the two countries found it difficult to come to an agreement on a common national anthem. For a while a translation of the British Royal Anthem was in use.

In Sweden a song by Carl Wilhelm August Strandberg (1818 to 1877) was sung with a tune by Otto Lindblad (1809–1864), the founder of the country's choral society for men. It begins *"Ur Svenska hjertans djup en gång"* ("From deep in Sweden's heart one time"). The tune is pleasant enough, but somehow it is not representative and has failed to win popular favor. For a while it served as the royal anthem in public ceremonies.

Much more characteristic is the anthem, *"Du gamla, du fria, du fjällhöga Nord"* ("Thou ancient, unconquered, thou rock-towered North").

It was written by the ethnologist Richard Dybeck (1811–1877) for a traditional popular melody which he had heard in the middle of the nineteenth century in Västmanland in Central Sweden. It cannot be so very old, for its modern tonality points to a period not earlier than the beginning of the nineteenth century. But it is dignified and in an arrangement for several voices it produces a memorable effect:

Its use as a national anthem dates back to the end of the nineteenth century. The complete first stanza reads:

Du gamla, du fria, du fjällhöga Nord
Du tysta, du glädjerika, sköna!
Jag hälsar dig vänaste land uppå jord,
Din sol, din himmel, dina ängder gröna.

(Thou ancient, unconquered, thou rock-towered North,
Thou quiet, thou blithesome, o thou fairest.
I praise thee the best of lands on the earth,
Thy sun, thy sky, and the verdure thou bearest.)

A song frequently used with the functions of an anthem is finally, *"Sverige, Sverige, fosterland"* ("Sweden, Sweden, my fatherland"), which was written by Verner von Heidenstam (1859–1940) and set to music in 1905 by Wilhelm Stenhammar (1871–1927).

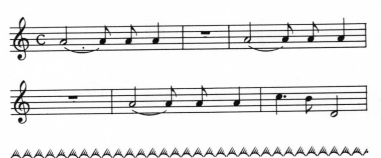

Norway has two national anthems. The more important one is *"Ja vi elsker dette landet"* ("Truly do we love this country") by Björnstjerne Björnson with music by Rikard Nordraak. Nothing need be said here about its famous author. Nordraak, a cousin of Björnson's, was born on June 12, 1842, in Oslo. He died on May 20, 1866, in Berlin. He was one of the first to let his art draw from the source of Norway's folk songs. Grieg thought of him as his model when he created his national Norwegian style.

The "Norse Fatherland Song" was first published as a poem on October 1, 1859, with a dedication to the King. The music was probably composed in 1863 or 1864. The first public recital of the anthem was given on May 17, 1864, on the occasion of the fiftieth anniversary of the Norwegian constitution.

The second Norwegian anthem is the song, *"Sønner af Norge det aeldgamle Rige"* ("Children of Norway, the age-honored realm"), by Henrik Bjerregaard. It was set to music by Christian Blom (1782–1861) who was not a professional musician but earned his living as the director of an insurance company in Oslo. The tune is not at all bad, and many a professional composer would feel proud if he had something like it among his productions.

One of the factors explaining the popularity of this tune is again the aesthetic appeal of the familiar. A song whose every phrase seems somehow a dear old acquaintance will always be welcome to the average listener.

The official National and Royal Anthem of **Denmark** is *"Kong Christian stod ved højen Mast"* ("King Christian stood by the lofty mast"). However, just as the United States and many other countries have "unofficial" anthems, so Denmark's *"Der er et yndigt Land"* ("There is a winsome Land") is a popular expression of everyday patriotism.

The words of "King Christian" were written by Johannes Ewald as part of his ballad opera *Fiskerne (The Fisherman)*, the music for which was composed by Johan Hartman, leader of the Royal Theater orchestra. However, when the ballad opera was first performed on January 31, 1780, only the last stanza was sung and that by no means with the tune now associated with the song. Actually, the ultimate origin of that tune is unknown and still a matter of dispute. It dates at least as far back as the years between 1762 and 1777, at which time it is found in a manuscript collection of violin music brought together by two musically inclined divinity students, the brothers Christian Frederik and Poul Danckel Bast, who made no reference to the composer's name (possibly unknown to them too). In 1785, the same melody appeared in a collection of community songs edited by Niels Schirring. Four years later the same Schirring brought out a collection of arias and songs from ballad operas including Ewald's "King Christian" from *The Fisherman*. Now the tune for the song as given in Schirring's collection was not at all taken from *The Fisherman*. It was an arrangement of the tune we have traced in the manuscript of the Bast brothers and Schirring's collection of community songs. But this arrangement was — by Hartmann himself, who thus deserves credit for having *found* the right tune for the song even though he was not — as popularly assumed —. the creator of it.

Hartmann's version was not in all respects identical with that current today. It was the popular German composer of sonatas and sonatinas for the pianoforte, Friedrich Kuhlau (1786–1832), who put the final touches to the song when he included it in 1828 in his setting of Heiberg's music drama, *Elverhøj* (Hill of the Elves). It had been similarly employed in at least two other operatic works but it seems that Kuhlau's use of it as the climax of his famous overture paved its way to fame and universal popular favor in all parts of Denmark.

Musically speaking the Danish anthem is one of the best. It represents the heroic type of the eighteenth century and bears some slight resemblance to "Rule Britannia."

In Denmark the tune is occasionally ascribed to Judge L. D. Rogert of Bornholm who was a friend of the poet Ewald. There is no proof in support of this theory which was first advanced in 1840 by the folk-song editor A. P. Berggreen.

Adam Oehlenschläger's twelve-stanza poem, *"Der er et yndigt Land"* ("There is a winsome land"), was written about 1819. It was set to music by Hans Ernst Kryer, but it was not well received during the early part of its history. Its great moment came on July 4, 1844, when students sang it at the national festival meeting on the Skamlingsbanken, before a crowd of 12,000 Danish patriots. From then on its rise in popularity was undisputed.

The melody begins as follows:

Iceland has a national anthem of its own which is in keeping with the country's status as a sovereign island republic. However, it was written and composed as early as 1874, the year when the Icelanders under the leadership of Jón Sigurdsson at last — after a thirty years' struggle — secured their own constitution which gave legislative powers to the Icelandic Althingi or diet but kept the country within the domain of the Kingdom of Denmark. It was also the year when Iceland celebrated the one thousandth anniversary of what is commonly regarded as the first permanent settlement of Europeans on the island. This event, the arrival of

Ingolf Arnason with a band of Norwegian followers in the year 874, is the inspiration of the Icelandic anthem which contains hardly an allusion to the political developments of the period of its origin.

The poet, Reverend Matthias Jochumsson (1835–1920), merged his theme with the Biblical *"Fyrir þér er einn dagur sem þúsund ár"* ("With Thee is one day as a thousand years") and stressed it in the refrain *"Islands þúsund ár"* ("Iceland's thousand years"). Jochumsson made also a name for himself as the translator into Icelandic of various plays by Shakespeare, Ibsen, and others. His original works include likewise a number of dramatic pieces.

The composer, Sveinbjörn Sveinbjörnsson (1847–1926), spent the greater part of his life in Edinburgh, Scotland, where he made a living as a music teacher. His anthem earned him a gold medal but it is difficult to discover in it anything strikingly Nordic. It is a competent but fairly conventional piece of work.

The national anthem of **Ireland** is "The Soldiers Song." It was officially adopted in July, 1926. The text is by Peader Kearney. This same Kearney collaborated with Patrick Heaney on the musical setting. The exact date of the composition cannot be ascertained. The words were written late in 1909 or early in 1910 and apparently first published in 1912 in *Irish Freedom*, a monthly expressing the views of the Irish Republican Brotherhood. The music of the anthem was composed not later than July, 1911, when Patrick Heaney died.

The tune has pentatonic elements and Scotch snaps which relate it clearly to Irish folk music but the national elements in it appear to be somewhat watered down by a modernizing tendency.

THE PENINSULAS OF SOUTHERN EUROPE

Italy, God's country of music, has never had a fully and officially established national anthem if we leave out of consideration the *"Giovinezza"* which was sung during the Fascist era. As in the case of Germany, the explanation may be found in Italy's national disruption of long standing. For a while the people had to get along with the *"Marcia reale"* ("Royal March") of 1834. During the stormy period of 1858, it is true, the Italians did produce a song that might pass muster as a sort of national anthem. This was the period of Cavour's political triumphs, of his idea that the country must reinstate the highest goals of the *risorgimento* and attain its reunion under the rule of the House of Savoy. The inspired words of Luigi Mercantini served the military bandleader Alessio Olivieri (1830—1867) as the basis for his typically Italian melody. It combines the highfalutin bombast of an Italian opera aria with the vim and vigor of a military march.

The first to sing the new anthem were the volunteers of the *Alpini* corps. They also gave it the name, *"Inno di guerra dei cacciatori delle Alpi"* ("Battle Hymn of Alpine Huntsmen"). But the song's great popularity dates from the world-renowned expedition of the one thousand Redshirts whom Garibaldi in 1860 led from Genoa to Marsala in Sicily, where he landed on May 11, proclaiming himself dictator and overthrowing the Bourbons in Naples.

From then on the song was known as the *"Inno di Garibaldi."* Wherever foreign intruders were to be made aware of the people's determined opposition, the "Garibaldi Anthem" was sung with national fury. The catchword, *"Va fuora d'Italia"* ("Get out of Italy"), was shouted a thousand and one times; it was hurled at the Austrians in Southern Tirol and in Trieste, also throughout Dalmatia, and at the French in Nice. Quite characteristically, the opening phrase of the anthem reads, *"All'armi..."* ("To arms..."). This operatic introduction is followed by a fiery march which would seem to have served as the model for many a Latin-American anthem.

> *All'armi, all'armi!*
> *Si scopron le tombe, si levano i morti,*
> *I martiri nostri son tutti risorti;*
> *Le spade nel pugno, gli allori alle chiome,*
> *La fiamma ed il nome d'Italia nel cor!...*

> (To arms, ye! To arms ye!
> The tombs have burst open, the dead have arisen,
> The martyrs we mourned have rejoined our column!
> Our fists clench the sword, our heads shine in laurel,
> And Italy's fire and her name fill our hearts!...)

But the "Garibaldi Anthem" was considered less a generally Italian than a specifically democratic song. It called up the memory of the humanitarian ideals of the *risorgimento* which had embodied a considerable portion of masonic thought.

The *"Marcia reale,"* on the other hand, composed as it was by Gabelli, could at best qualify as second-rate music and was hardly fit to serve as a source of inspiration and national fervor. Its opening phrases run thus:

Under the Fascist rule in Italy a new anthem had to be secured. It was found in *"Giovinezza,"* the *"Canto dei Fascisti"* ("Youth, the Song of the Fascists"). The words were by Marcello Manni, the music by G. Castaldo who acknowledged the use of certain motives by G. Blanc. The refrain,

> *Giovinezza, giovinezza,*
> *Primavera de bellezza*

hastily rendered as

> Juvenescence, juvenescence,
> Of all beauty spring and essence,

shows a depressing lack of originality. It is little more than a paraphrase of the German student song, *"Drum ade, ade"* ("Now farewell, farewell"). When Toscanini refused to conduct a per= formance of the *"Giovinezza,"* he was doubtless moved by political considerations; but his musical objections to the Fascist anthem were as strong if not stronger and quite enough to justify his attitude. After the collapse of the Fascist regime, the functions of an Italian national anthem were taken over for a while by the "Garibaldi Anthem" and the "International."

When the Italian Republic emerged from the turmoil following the second World War, it had no official national anthem. Un= officially the *Inno di Mameli* came to be used. It gets its name from the author of the text, the poet and patriot Goffredo Mameli (1827–1849). It begins,

> *Fratelli d'Italia,*
> *L'Italia s'è desta...*
>
> (Brothers of Italia,
> Italia is awake...)

and proceeds in a vein of fairly aggressive patriotism which claims that God created victory as a servant of the fatherland. Mameli wrote this battle hymn in November 1847. In 1848 he served as a volunteer under Garibaldi in Lombardy and in 1849 became chief of staff of the Roman Republic. The *"Fratelli d'Italia"* was set to music almost immediately by Michele Novaro, and through= out Italy it helped awaken interest in the growing revolutionary movement. The tune begins as follows:

The march has a forceful introduction, marked *andante maestoso*, in triplet rhythms which are carried throughout the entire first section in the accompaniment. The vocal line itself has an energetic motive of dotted eighths evidently intended to symbolize the marching Italians. The same motive is carried through the middle section of the anthem, which modulates to the subdominant, after which it returns to the main key.

Musically, the *"Inno di Mameli"* — like the *"Inno di Garibaldi"* — belongs to the category of marchlike anthems which are so charac= teristic of the South American countries.

♫♫♫♫♫♫♫♫♫♫♫♫♫♫♫♫♫♫♫♫♫♫♫♫♫♫♫♫

The **Vatican** has an official Papal anthem, although there is no text to go with it. This "Marcia Pontificale" was composed by Charles Gounod for the coronation of Pope Pius IX in 1846. More than a century later, in 1949, it was given official recognition as the Papal anthem.

♫♫♫♫♫♫♫♫♫♫♫♫♫♫♫♫♫♫♫♫♫♫♫♫♫♫♫♫

Spain has likewise a "Royal March." Its origin is disputed. There are those who claim that it was composed by a German and that King Frederick the Great handed it in 1770 as a gift for King Charles III (1759–1788) to Count Aranda who had come to Berlin to study the organization of the Prussian army. By royal decree of September 3, 1770, it was officially recognized as a "March of Honor."

According to another tradition the tune was originally French and was brought to Spain by Philip V (1701–1746). It became popular under the name of *"Marcha Grenadera."* Then, under Charles III (1759–1788), the court oboist Espinosa reset it for military orchestras after the model of the type of march in vogue under Frederick the Great. Ever since it has been played at all court celebrations and also during Mass when the Holy Wafer was exhibited. It has been used in military reviews as well. It is rather slow — about sixty paces a minute — and makes a solemn rather than a fiery impression.

At times the *"Himno del Ciudadano Riego"* ("Anthem of Citizen Riego") takes the place of the lacking national anthem. The words — *"Soldados, la patria nos clama a la lid"* ("O soldiers, the country now calls us to the fray") — were written in 1812 by Colonel Riego at Algeciras when he and his battalion "Asturias" resisted embar= kation to the colonies. The trite tune went originally with another text. During the Spanish Republic (1931–1936), the *"Himno de Riego"* was adapted as the national anthem. When Franco rose to power, the "Royal March" came to the fore again.

It is interesting to note that in 1870 King Amadeo I invited public competition for a Spanish national anthem. The prize he offered was considerable, but none of the 447 contestants was crowned with success, and the old royal march remained in force. It is strange that it shows no trace of Spanish folklore, but in its simplicity and especially through its somewhat archaic concluding phrases it is the musical symbol of the *grandeza* of the Spanish people.

It is a well-known historical fact that many a cultural institution came to the Iberian peninsula from South America. Folk songs and dances were thus imported and thus the **Portuguese** national anthem was brought over from Brazil. But what makes this an absolutely unique case is the fact that the King himself wrote the anthem of Portugal for himself and his people.

When Pedro I on the heights of Ipiranga near São Paolo severed on September 7, 1822, the bonds that linked Brazil to Portugal and had himself proclaimed emperor, he wrote in the interest of his popularity the anthem, *"O Patria, o Rei, o Povo"* ("O Father= land, o King, o People"). When in 1826, after the death of King John VI of Portugal, he himself ascended the Portuguese throne, he took the anthem with him and had it introduced as the national anthem of the old country. His successors kept it under the name of *"Himno da Carta."* In its contents it is as well a royal as a democratic anthem and simultaneously a religious song as well.

Since 1910, a patriotic song entitled *"A Portuguêsa"* ("The Portuguese") has been in use in Portugal. The words are by Lopez de Mendonça (about 1890), the music by Alfredo Keil (1850—1907), a Portuguese composer and exponent of Portuguese music, who was of German extraction and died in Hamburg after having written the first Portuguese grand opera, *Serrana*. *"A Portuguêsa"* begins thus:

THE BALKANS

The Serbs, Croats, and Slovenes had their own national anthems before their countries merged to form the kingdom of **Yugoslavia**. The Serbs sang *"Bože pravde, Ti, što spase"* ("God of justice, hast preserved..."), a song written by J. Djordjewič and put to music by Davorin Jenko. The Croats sang *"Lijepa naša domovino"* ("Our fair country") with words by Anton Mihanovič (1835) and music by Josip Runjanin (1846). The Slovenes, finally, sang *"Naprey zastava Slave"* ("Forward, arise, Slav").

After World War I the opening passages of these three anthems were more or less skilfully patched together. The last line of the Serb anthem was appended and lo! there was the Yugoslav anthem, a musical symbol of the union of three peoples. How successful a product it turned out to be from a musical point of view remains of course somewhat questionable. It begins thus:

In 1945 Yugoslavia became a republic and the old anthem, the "King's Anthem," had to be dropped for political reasons. For the same type of reason it had not enjoyed much popularity throughout the preceding years. A suitable text for a new anthem was found in a poem by Cedomir Minderovic. Its title was "Our Republic," but the problem of the right melody to go with it remained some= how unsolved. For a while, during the early years of Marshal Tito's regime, the "International" was sung in lieu of a regular national anthem. More and more frequently, however, the function of investing state celebrations and other festive occasions with the proper musical garb was entrusted to the Pan-Slavic hymn (in Serb beginning *"Hej Slaveni"*) which will be discussed in its proper con= text.

The **Bulgarians** have a very simple anthem. It is a march trio and begins *"Schumi Maritza okărwawena"* ("Foaming Maritza, blood-tainted waters"). The Maritza is the most important river of Bulgaria. The anthem was written by Nikolo Schiwkow (1847 to 1901). The music was composed by Gabriel Šebek, a Czech conductor who had gone to live in Bulgaria but who returned at a later period to Prague. The historian of music Bohn reports that the publisher Zimmerman remembered having met Šebek as late as 1904. No further details about his life have been recorded.

The tune is by no means original. It is almost identical with the trio of the bravura piano piece, "The Awakening of the Lion," by Antoine de Koutski (1816—1899) which was very popular at the time of its publication about 1850. The German soldier's song, *"Wenn die Soldaten durch die Stadt marschieren"* ("When our soldiers march along the pavement"), has also the same beginning. There is no trace of Bulgarian folklore in this anthem; as a matter of fact, there is nothing Slavic in it. It is just a rather trite pop= ular tune of German origin. Still, it is not hard to understand why the Bulgarians should be extremely proud of their "Maritza" which was recognized as the official anthem in 1885. Up to that time they had used the Russian anthem as a patriotic song.[9]

The national anthems of the Balkan countries are not especially original — an observation which applies also to the anthem of **Rumania.** In 1861 public competition was invited for a sort of reception flourish in honor of Prince Alexandru Ioan Cuza (1820 to 1873) who in 1859 had been elected prince of Moldavia and Wa= lachia and whom the Turks had recognized as the ruler of the united principalities of Rumania. The contest was won by Eduard A. Huebsch (1833–1894), a military band leader of Jassy. After Alexandru's abdication, when the Hohenzollerns succeeded to the throne, one Vasile Alexandri adapted the text, which was a fairly conventional glorification of the ruler, to suit the new king, Carol I. Huebsch was quite successful with his anthem. He advanced to the position of inspector general of military music in Rumania with the rank of major.

The anthem known as *"Trăiască Regele"* ("Long live the King"), shows German traits and is not bad as music although it is certainly pieced together. The beginning is identical with Kuhlau's *"Duo brillant"* (op. 110 b), and the arpeggios are conventional phrases of the kind frequently encountered in German popular music.

After the proclamation of the Rumanian People's Republic on December 30, 1947, a "Hymn dedicated to the People's Republic" by Aurel Baranga was set to music by Matei Socor.

It was not intended as a permanent solution of the problem of the Rumanian national anthem and subsequently has not proved to be one.

The "definitive anthem" goes back to 1953 and was the result of a contest in which the same Socor was awarded first prize. The words were written by Eugene Frunza and Dan Desliu. The music has certainly more personality than that of many other recent anthems, but there is little in it that could impress us as Rumanian. The first stanza reads:

> Land of the fathers, Rumania, lofty and high.
> Over thy peaceful fields rises thy sky.
> The yoke of the past was condemned, and it fell.
> Not in vain did the elders find force to rebel.
> Our work shall complete what their visions foretell.
>
> Refrain:
> Free now, firmly in its hands
> The Republic of the People
> Of Rumania holds its fate.
> May it live and prosper.

The **Albanian** anthem was composed in 1880 by the Rumanian conductor Ciprian Porumbescu in Czernowitz. The text, selected through a contest, is likewise by a Rumanian, Andrei Bărseanu. The opening measures are as follows:

There is a marked resemblance between the *Viva*-phrase of the Portuguese anthem and certain aspects of the anthem of **Greece**. On second thought, this fact is not so very surprising, for early in the nineteenth century all second and third-rate musicians shared one common influence: that of the opera. For this reason numerous anthems — including those of the South American Republics — sound as though they had been borrowed from Italian operas.

Greece may claim to have the longest national anthem in the world. It has no fewer than one hundred and fifty-eight stanzas of four lines each. It reminds one strikingly of those Yugoslav and Macedonian folk songs of the ballad variety which sing the story of ancestral heroes to the accompaniment of the gusla, a rudimen= tary guitarlike instrument of the Balkan countries. The poet of the Greek anthem, Dionysios Solomós, was born in 1798 on the island of Zante and died in 1857 in Corfu. In his anthem, written in 1823, he sang the heroic deeds of the Greek fighters for freedom, the fall of Tripolis, the battle of Corinth, the defense of Missolonghi, the first sea encounters, and the tragic end of the patriarch Grigorios in Constantinople.

King George I of Greece declared the poem Greece's national anthem. For this purpose it was naturally shortened. The composer was Nicolaos Manzaros (1795–1873). He had studied in Italy and earned the first successes of his career there. If one did not know about this, it certainly could be inferred from his "Hymn to Free= dom" of 1828 which shows no Hellenic characteristics but is pronouncedly Italian.

The Greeks were not quite certain that their anthem was musi= cally adequate. So, at the suggestion of King Otto, it was sub= mitted to musical experts in Bavaria. When no veto was forth= coming, a special edict bestowed official standing upon the anthem in 1864. The sense of the first stanza is about as follows:

> Never shall I fail to know thee
> By the fire of thine eye,
> As the world is ranged below thee
> And thy sword is raised on high.
> From the sacred soil of Hellas
> Thou hast risen valiantly.
> May thy strength again impel us,
> Precious Freedom, hail to thee!

EASTERN EUROPE

During the first World War, **Polish** legions fought in Italy side by side with the Allies. They were fighting for the cause of their Polish fatherland. And indeed, one cannot help being deeply moved when one considers that in singing their national anthem they found in its text a perfect description of the state they were in:

> Poland will not be forsaken
> While we live to love her.
> What the foe from us has taken
> Let the sword recover.
>
> > From Italian soil, Dombrowski,
> > Back to Poland lead us.
> > In thy guard are trusting
> > We and all that heed us.
>
> Poles ahead are boldly crossing
> Vistula and Warta.
> How the foe is to be beaten
> Learn from Bonaparte.
>
> > From Italian soil, Dombrowski,
> > Back to Poland lead us.
> > In thy guard are trusting
> > We and all that heed us . . .

From generation to generation the Poles have kept their firm faith in a future rebirth of their country. The Polish anthem is a symbol of this faith.

After the third partition of Poland, in 1795, when Prussia, Russia, and Austria had swallowed up the country which had been weakened by internal troubles, the Polish patriots looked to France as the savior in their hour of greatest need. It was then that Polish legions were formed within the French revolutionary armies, partic= ularly on Italian soil and through the initiative of General Jan Henryk Dombrowski (1755—1818) who had previously made a name for himself by taking part in Kosciuszko's revolt of 1794. It was in Italy in 1797 that the Polish national anthem was sung for the first time.

Both the words and the music are by General Józef Wybicki (1747—1822), but we must add that a good case is made by those who prefer to ascribe the music to Michael K. Oginski (1765—1833). The tune is typically Polish. It is a mazurka whose rhythm, ♫ ♩ ♩ is of course perfect for a march as well.

In course of time the name of Dombrowski was replaced by other national heroes and dictators and the words were corre= spondingly altered. During the Polish revolution, it was the name of General Józef Chlopicki (1772—1854) which appeared in the refrain. Chlopicki was the dictator of Poland from December, 1830, to January, 1831. The following year it was the turn of General Jan Skrzynecki (1787—1860). He lost the battle of Ostrolenka and 8,000 men, and naturally his name disappeared from the anthem about as fast as that of Chlopicki. A text written by Stefan Wit= wicki was likewise short-lived. Finally the song was re-established and sung in its original version. At the end of both World Wars, Poland celebrated the advent of what seemed at the time final and permanent liberation by instituting the Dombrowski anthem as the country's official national anthem.

In the course of the nineteenth century the Polish anthem came to be an unofficial Czech anthem too. The text was of course dif= ferent. It began: *„Hej Slované, ješte naše slovanská řeč žíje"* ("Ho you Slavs, the Slavic tongue is still alive").

The tune underwent some modifications too, and it is not devoid of interest to compare the original Polish with the later Czech versions.

Dombrowski Anthem:

Hej Slované:

The Czech tune seems harder and more compact. It reflects a more aggressive spirit than the softer Polish original. This is quite apparent at the very start where the Polish diatonic series appears in Czech replaced by a clarion-like triad in keeping with the war cry, "Ho you Slavs." The hardening of the originally mellow and in a sense resigned tune corresponds with the more determined spirit of the Czech nation and also with the quality of the Czech language which is rich in consonants and spurts forth its vowels with a resulting clear-cut and staccato-like rhythm.

"Hej Slované" became the song oft the pan-Slavic movement, in particular of the Slavic Irredenta in Austria which during the realm of Emperor Francis Joseph (1848–1917) had its center in Prague. In the Austrian Monarchy it was strictly forbidden to sing this song. As a result the Czechs sang it only the more. Thousands of Czechs defied imprisonment and other forms of punishment by singing the *"Hej Slované"* — a battle song in the best sense of the term — during their pan-Slavic congresses and on the occasion of all their various *Sokol* festivals. When these determined and war= like men — their fists clenched — sang their *"Hrom a peklo / Marně vaše proti nám, sou vzteky"* ("Death and Hell! Vain is your hate against us"), whoever heard and saw them knew that Old Austria's death knell would soon be sounded.

The second Polish anthem has no less interesting a history. It has often been sung under the title of "Polish Prayer" and begins, *"Bože coš Polske przez tak liezne wieki."* The text is by A. Felinski (1771–1820) and the melody by K. Kurpinski (1785–1857).

With a spiritual text the tune was dedicated in 1815 to Emperor Alexander I of Russia and included in the official church hymnal and prayer book. Somewhat later the same tune was forbidden throughout Poland on penalty of death, and in 1866 a resolution was passed at the episcopal synod of Gniezno to strike it from the hymnal.

The song fully deserves the title of honor often bestowed upon it, that is, the Polish Anthem of the Opposition. But those who consider it a typically Polish tune in which the spirit of Poland pulsates go more than a little too far. Actually the melody goes back to the French operetta *le Secret* by Jean Pierre Solié and was written in 1796 or 1797.

This Solié was an interesting musician. He began his career in Paris as a tenor at the *Comédie Italienne.* At first he sang with indifferent success, but all this changed when his voice turned into a beautiful baritone, for up to this time baritones were completely unknown for comic-opera parts. Now composers began writing parts specifically for Solié's voice, and he was the hero of the day. As for his own operettas, the one called *The Secret* accompanied him on his tours all over Europe and got as far as Poland. And it seems that Kurpinski, normally a rather talented and original composer of Polish dances, could think of nothing better than the aria, *"Qu'on soit jalouse"* when he found himself confronted with the assignment to compose a tune for the anthem of the opposition. The beginning of the aria reads roughly, "Let jealousy pervade their feelings; it helps to fan the flame of love," and the corresponding tune is:

Still today this melody is heard in Upper Silesia. Likewise in the diocese of Olomouc where — according to Jaroslav Vavřik's little volume, *Lidová Píseň ve Slezsku* — the words are *"Bože, cos račil před tisíce lety,"* a Czech translation of the Polish text.

During the first World War — and under Hitler, for that matter, too — German soldiers sang the song with the words, *"Zehn= tausend Mann, die zogen ins Manöver"* ("Ten thousand men were marching in maneuvers"), and at least one edition of a *German Song Book for Public Schools (Gesangbuch für Bürgerschulen,* Reichenberg, 1924), included it with the explicit warning, "lively and spirited *(flott und lustig)* and not after the sentimental fashion of the Poles."

So this anthem too is typically a migrating melody. There is an Italian folk song with the text, *"Vien qua Dorina bella, vien qua ti vo abbracciar"* ("Come here, my fair Dorina, I want you in my arms"). The tune is:

Carl Maria von Weber wrote masterly variations on the theme. In Zoellner's piano manual we find a "Canzonetta" by a certain Bianchi:

And so we could go on illustrating the same point. But it may be more interesting to devote a few paragraphs to the third Polish popular anthem which owes its existence to the revolt of 1863.

Czar Alexander II had initiated a Polish policy of concessions. In 1862 he appointed the Polish count Alexander Wielopolski gov= ernor in his Polish kingdom. But the "reds" — then a designation for the Polish patriots — considered this development a grave danger for the national idea, for Wielopolski advocated Poland's definitive abandonment of all claims to its former territories east of the Niemen and Bug rivers, which Russia looked upon as genuinely Russian lands. So the "reds" began fomenting unrest throughout Congress Poland, and in 1863 it flared up in open rebellion. The new anthem was written by H. Ujeski. The composer was J. Nikorowicz. It begins, "Z dymen pażarów z kurzem krwi bratniej." The melody in minor is characteristically nostalgic. A peculiarity of its first part is the descending Phrygian mode which points to an age-old ancestry. Such tunes are found in the Orient and Old Spain where many a Polish melody has more or less striking blood relations.

The Polish anthems are clearly among the most interesting popular anthems of the world.

The Bohemians had a sort of national anthem as far back as the later Middle Ages. I am thinking of course of the famous battle song "Kdož iste Boží bojovníci" ("You, the fighters of the Lord"), of the followers of Jan Hus, the great Czech reformer. This song — not unlike Luther's "Ein feste Burg ist unser Gott" ("A mighty fortress is our Lord") — has filled multitudes with religious enthusiasm and was a source of awe and fear for the German crusaders. In later times Smetana used it as the leitmotiv of his symphonic poem *Tabor,* and Dvořák made of it the theme of his *Husitska:*

The official national anthem of the **Czechs,** however, is the melodious song, "*Kde domov muj.*" Like "Rule Brittania," the

Czech anthem was originally an operatic melody. Its first per= formance occurred on December 21, 1834, as part of the operetta *Fidlovačka (The Fair)*. The librettist was the reputed Czech poet Jan Kajetan Tyl; the composer František Škroup (1801—1862). Both men are representatives of the Czech national renaissance, the reawakening of the soul of the Czech people. Škroup was a noteworthy composer who held the position of second conductor from 1827 and that of first conductor from 1837 to 1857 at the National Theater in Prague. He spent his last years as conductor at the Opera in Rotterdam. His operas were written partly in German, partly in Czech. Two of them have recently been revived. *Dráteník (The Tinker)* was first performed in 1826. Its score was actually published in a piano arrangement. The same holds true for *Fidlovačka*. Both mirror the mind and soul of the simple Czech citizen of the era before 1848. They illustrate the profound gulf which separated the members of the German aristocracy and bourgeoisie representing at the time the highest social classes in Prague and Bohemia from the small Czech craftsman and farmer whose national awakening began to manifest itself in contemporary Czech art.

When the *Fidlovačka* was performed for the first time, no one could have foreseen that its number 19 would play a great part in the history of the Czech people. In the operetta the blind minstrel Mareš sings this song in praise of the beauties of the Czech countryside and the simple and natural friendliness of the Czech people. It was a simple song and had none of the sweetly romantic undertone which later generations have read into it. At the same time it is a typical and genuine operetta song and starts and closes with an orchestral passage in conventional eighths. Its rise in pop- ular favor was accelerated when the two singers, Karel Strakatý (1804—1868) and Jan K. Piška (1814—1873), made it a frequent item on their programs. The *Fidlovačka* as a whole, however, was forgotten and the manuscript seemed lost. But it was recovered and the operetta was produced again on July 9, 1917.

As holds true for most songs which are close to a people's heart, the *"Kde domov muj"* developed its own cycle of legends. There is for instance the story that Škroup had composed it at the deathbed of his wife. A touching story, but it was spoiled when overzealous researchers ascertained that the wife of the composer, Wilhelmine, nee Koudelková, died only in 1838.

In its lyrical mellowness, its romantic dulcitude, the song is a perfect expression of the peaceful and somewhat sentimental qualities of the Czech people. What a contrast to the bellicose song of the Hussites. There are some critics who claim that the *"Kde domov muj"* is not in all its phrases completely original. As a matter of fact, the phrase

does reveal a pronounced resemblance to the major theme of Mozart's *Sinfonie Concertante.*

But all this can merely show once again that it makes really no difference whatever how original a tune actually is. This melody was accepted by the entire people as its property and so it is truly a folk song. The operatic prelude was forgotten. The tune itself underwent certain minor changes in keeping with the phenomenon of "wearing down and singing down" which characterizes the true folk song, and today, when the song is sung, no one will think of either its composer or the *Fidlovačka* from which it stems.

During the Austrian rule, the *"Kde domov muj"* was next to the *"Hej Slované"* a sort of pacific protest song against the foreign overlords. In 1919 it became the authentic national anthem of the Czechs and was sung together with the Slovak anthem, *"Nad Tatrou sa blyska"* ("On Tatra Mountains lightning . . ."). The text

of this latter song was an adaptation produced in 1844 by Janko
Matuška. Its melody is of the kind one finds with variations in
many countries. It runs:

and is clearly reminiscent for instance of the Hungarian folk song,
"Szöke kis lany" ("Lass a-fetching water").

Of course the passage of melodies and melody fragments across
ethnological and political boundaries is very common, and we must
not forget that Slovakia stood for a long time under Hungarian
rule and that Hungarians lived in Slovakia as Slovaks did in
Hungary.

The characerological difference between Czechs and Slovaks is
clearly indicated in their national anthems. The Czechs incline
toward the West while the Slovaks, whose country borders on
the Ukraine and hence on Russia, exhibit a strongly Eastern orien=
tation. Indeed, from a musical point of view there is nothing more
interesting than a trip from Bohemia to Slovakia. The Czechs in
Bohemia sing folk songs in major. The farther east we go the rarer
are folk songs in major. This begins to be true in Moravia, and in
Slovakia most folk songs are in minor. Hence we are not surprised
to find that the Czech national anthem is written in major, the
Slovak anthem in minor. Yet, however different the two melodies
may be, their juxtaposed performance is quite harmonious.
Through their contrast the two songs form a union, and musically

speaking (and politically too) the Czecho-Slovak anthems must be regarded as a more felicitous solution than the Yugoslav arrangement in which the anthems of the three peoples of the nation are intertwined.

The "Hej Slované" which the Czechs used to sing as a pan-Slavic anthem and a radical battle song against Austrian rule has been discussed in connection with the Polish national anthem.

Czarist **Russia** had a beautiful and dignified national anthem, "Bože, carja chrani" ("God Save the Czar"). It had two officially recognized stanzas written by Vasili Andreevich Zhukovski. The first one was dated 1834; the second was actually the older and had been printed in 1814. Another version consisting of Zhukovski's stanza of 1814 plus two additional stanzas by the Russian poet Aleksander Sergeevich Pushkin did not meet with general approval.

The composer of the anthem was Aleksei Fëdorovich Lvov (1799–1870), amateur violinist and composer, Major General and Adjutant of Emperor Nicholas I. From 1836 to 1855 he was the conductor of the Imperial Choir at Court. With a number of operas and violin concertos as well as one Fantasy for violin and orchestra he was not too successful. In his time he was not entirely unknown as the author of choral compositions. In 1833 he wrote in compliance with the Czar's orders the anthem which assured him his humble niche in the pantheon of music. The melody is conceived in a truly dignified and homogeneous style, and in the company of the world's great anthems it is most definitely not out of place. Now when it is outlawed in Russia it can be heard in many an American church, and the University of Pennsylvania has adopted it as the official tune of its college song.

After the Bolshevist revolution the Czar's anthem was naturally abandoned. Its place was taken by the "International," the battle song of the international socialist labor movement. It was written in 1871 by Eugène Pottier, a member of the Paris Commune, whose songs of the revolution were collected in 1887 under the title of *Chants révolutionnaires*.

The tune of the "International" was written by a worker from Lille named Degeyter. At first authorship of Adolphe Degeyter was not contested. When the song became world-renowned, his brother Pierre Degeyter, a woodcarver by profession, claimed the honor of having composed the tune. The resulting lawsuit lasted eighteen years and ended with Pierre's victory. The tune is gen= erally known and certainly most attractive:

As long as Russia identified itself explicitly with the cause of World Revolution, the "International" was regarded as a battle song against international capitalism, which could not be too pleasant for a number of other nations including the Western democracies. When the USSR joined these democracies in their battle against Hitlerite Germany, the "International" was no longer "the thing to sing" for the Russians. At the close of the year 1943, the "Anthem of the Soviet Union" was consequently produced. The words were by Sergei Mikhalkov and Elj-Registan. They speak of the Russian Republics as a proud fatherland united in freedom and power to form a bulwark of friendship for nation and men. The music was composed by A. V. Aleksandrov (d. 1946).[10] It is forceful and musically well done. It appeals to the taste of the Russian soldier who has always been known to sing it enthu= siastically.

Hungary has a very ancient national tune, the "Rákóczy March," which formerly took the place of a national anthem. The march was named after Francis Rákóczy (1676–1735). In the years 1700 and 1701, Rákóczy tried to enlist French support for a Hungarian insurrection against the Hapsburgs. He was arrested by the Austrians and committed to prison in Wiener-Neustadt. With his wife's help he made an adventurous escape to Poland. In 1703, a peasant uprising in Upper Hungary gave him his cue to start a movement of national liberation in earnest. In course of time he was elected ruler of Hungary. But the bliss of Hungarian independence was short-lived. Rákóczy's own general, Károlyi, made peace with the Austrians in 1711. From then on Rákóczy lived in exile in France and Turkey. The march which still bears his name is supposed to have been his favorite piece of music. It has proved its power to carry men away in flaming enthusiasm not only where Hungarians were involved. The current arrangement is the work of Wenzel Ružička who died in 1823. According to Aladár von Tóth, in Adler's *Handbuch der Musikgeschichte*, Johann Bihari (1764–1827) gave final shape to the march.

Various composers, among them Liszt and Berlioz, made use of the tune in their works. Berlioz in particular gave it world fame by introducing it in *la Damnation de Faust* (1846). He had Faust appear in Hungary to watch a Hungarian army marching across the distant plains. At this point the Rákóczy March is played. When the arrangement was performed in Budapest, Berlioz scored one of his most triumphant successes. What he had done was quite revolutionary at the time, and Hungarian journalists were frank in admitting that they had not considered it possible that a French composer could evolve a superior orchestral piece from a march which they held sacred as a national Hungarian possession. As a matter of fact, Berlioz himself, as he reported later on, was haunted by fears and worries as the hour of the performance ap= proached. His description of the première is extremely vivid. "After a trumpet call with the rhythm of the first measures of the melody, the theme itself is announced by flutes and clarinets and pizzicato strings. During this unwonted performance the audience remained calm and cold. But when the following drawn-out crescendo presented fugued portions of the theme with intermittent rum= blings of the big drum, the hall began to ferment in muted sounds which it is very hard to describe. And finally, as the orchestra — released in furious uproar — threw out the full force of its com= pressed fortissimo, an incredible outburst of shouting voices and stamping feet went trembling to the foundations of the building. The unanimous fury of all these fiery souls erupted in a fashion that sent shivers down my spine."

That is Berlioz' "Rákóczy March" seen through Hungarian temperaments. Still today Budapest concert audiences go wild when they hear it performed.

There have been numerous attempts to give the march a patriotic text. None has succeeded in getting both official recognition and popular approval. Under the Hapsburgs, the "Rákóczy March" was always regarded as revolutionary. The endeavor to introduce Haydn's anthem in Hungary too failed completely. It did gain a foothold in Croatia which was loyal to the Hapsburgs, but that was its extreme limit.

As for an anthem with official sanction, there was no such thing in Hungary up to 1842 when a public contest was organized for the purpose. The prize went to Franz Erkel, the distinguished Hun=

garian composer who lived from 1810 to 1893. He is considered the creator of the Hungarian national opera and of national Hungarian music as a public institution in general. He was the director of the Hungarian Academy of Music and organized the philharmonic concerts in Budapest. Various other musical institutions and organizations owe their existence to Erkel. His national operas, *Hunyady László* and *Bánk Bán*, and several of his symphonic poems — full of racy *"Hungarian"* music — are still very much alive.

Erkel's anthem is typically *"Hungarian"* in the sense which musical thinking ascribed to the term in the nineteenth century and in which it is still popularly understood. We should note at least in passing that since the time of Bartók the concepts of Hungarian folklore have completely changed, and compositions in the style of Erkel, Brahms, and Liszt are now considered written in *"Verbunkos"*, that is, a pseudo-Hungarian (gypsy) style.

The first edition of Erkel's anthem was published by the firm of Rószavoelgyi & Co. in Pest. It was arranged for male and female voices with piano accompaniment and bore merely the caption, "Anthem, Words by Franz Koelczey." The composer dedicated the work "with deep respect" to the congenial friend of the inspired poet, the Right Honorable Franz Deak. This was the famous leader of the Hungarian Liberal Reform Party whose policies led to the restoration of Hungary's constitution and the establishment of a political union between Austria and Hungary in the form of a dual monarchy.

In contrast to many other anthems, Erkel's work can withstand the strictest critical scrutiny. Wagner's dictum that a national anthem is a mirror of the people's character is fully borne out by it. It is both fiery and chivalrous. A certain rhetorical element does not prevent it from being strictly logical in structure. The most characteristic features of Hungarian popular music (as the nine=

teenth century saw it), are skilfully employed: the strangely syncopated rhythm which defies all attempts at translation; the sweeping runs of the cymbal; and finally in prelude and postlude the pounding tones of the tom-tom which produces a somewhat unexpected effect on non-Hungarian ears.

About the origin of Koelczey's poem, a note in the Rószavoelgyi edition gives the information, "from the tempestuous era of the Hungarian people, Czeke, January 22, 1823." Other authorities trace it back to 1817. The first two stanzas, untranslatable like all Hungarian poetry, have roughly the following sense:

> Bless, O Lord, supreme in might
> Hungary's confiding force.
> During the embattled night
> Shield her sons' victorious course.
> When their fateful lot seems cast,
> Let a blissful present last.
> Ample penance does the future
> And so did the past.
>
> Over the Carpathian heights
> Thou did'st guide their father's crews,
> Gav'st this land of rare delights
> To the seed of Bendeguz.
> By the Tisza's winding stream,
> By the Danube's verdant gleam,
> Arpad's sons lived lives of heroes,
> Peerless to beseem.

Hungary has a second national anthem, the so-called "Szózat" or "Salute". The words, written in 1836, are by Mihály Vörös= marty (1800—1855), a poet who is held in high esteem by the Hungarians. For a long time he was considered Hungary's greatest poet, principally by reason of his epic Zalán Futása (1824; The Flight of Zalan) which presents in classical form but pithy and poetic language a glorification of the Hungarian landscape. Vö=

rösmarty's poems are likewise pervaded by an ardent love of Hungary. In Budapest an imposing monument has been erected for him. The inscription in its base gives in lieu of the poet's name the first two lines of his "Szózat" which every Hungarian knows. The music was written by Benjamin Egressy (1814–1851) who made a name for himself not only as poet and musician but also as actor and singer. In his early years he had walked all the way to Milan in order to perfect himself as a singer. In later times he became choir conductor at the national theater in Budapest, but he was also active as a composer and librettist. In the latter capacity he wrote, for instance, the words for Erkel's national operas, among them for *Hunyady László*.

The score for the "Szózat" was published by the firm of *Rósza= voelgyi* in an arrangement for one voice with piano accompaniment and also for a male choir without accompaniment. All that has been said about Erkel's anthem may be applied to the "Szózat" as well. Its first two stanzas may be translated as follows:

Thy fatherland, O Magyar, claims
Thy love blameless and brave.
It rears and feeds and covers thee,
Thy cradle and thy grave.
In all far corners of the earth
No other hearth is thine.
Here thou must face thy fated lot,
Rise here and here decline.

This is the soil thy fathers' blood
Has drenched a hundredfold,
The soil which of a thousand years
Proud memories does hold.
Here Arpad's armies fought to stay,
Found hearth and home at length.
And here the yoke of serfdom fell
Through Hunyad's glorious strength.

Israel has an anthem whose goal and purpose it is to serve the renaissance of the Jewish people, the strengthening of its national reawakening, and the development of the promised land.

This anthem, the *"Hatikvah"* ("Hope"), is not merely used by the Jews of Israel. It unites all ethnically determined Jews through= out the world and was actually adopted as the Zionist anthem as long ago as 1897, the year of the first international Zionist Con= gress at Basel, Switzerland. The text was written by the itinerant Hebrew scholar and poet Naftali Herz Imber (1856—1909). Its original title was *"Tikvatenu"* ("Our Hope"). It was first published in the collection *Barkai (Morning Star)* which appeared in 1886 in Jerusalem where Imber lived at the time. The tune has been dis= cussed briefly in connection with other migrating melodies in our introductory chapter. Its notation is ascribed to Samuel Cohen, pioneer settler of Rishon le Zion in Israel. On the other hand, Peter Gradenwitz quotes in his book, *The Music of Israel* (1949), a personal acquaintance of Imber's to the effect that the latter had borrowed the tune from a cantorial composition by the famous Cantor Nissan Belzer. In any event, it does represent a type which has been familiar in Spanish folk singing for centuries. Pedrell, the well-known Spanish folklore expert, quotes a very similar tune under the title of *"Virgen de la Cueva"* ("Virgin of the Cave"). It would seem that the Sephardic Jews knew it in Spain and took it along with them to the Orient. It is interesting to note that the same tune can be found among the Poles (*"Pod Krakovem"*), the Basques, and even the Netherlanders.

The *"Hatikvah"* tune, now the official anthem of the State of Israel, runs as follows:

The first stanza of Imber's text reads in transliteration:

Kol od ba-le-vav pni-mah
Ne-fesh ye-hudee ho-mi-yah
Ul-fa-atei-miz-rach, ka-di-mah
A-yin l'tzi-on tzo-fi-yah . . .

(As long as still a Jewish heart
Beats in a Jewish breast,
As Jewish eyes in longing smart
To find in Zion rest . . .)

The Hashemite Kingdom of the **Jordan** is one of the several countries of the Middle East which use an orchestral piece of military flavor in lieu of a national anthem in the Western sense. In the case of the Kingdom of the Jordan it is a sort of royal salute of only ten measures. Its full effect must be imagined as resulting from a scoring for clarinets, flutes and piccolos, oboes, saxophones, cornets, and various sizes of saxhorns, together with drums and other percussion instruments.

The anthem was written about the time when Emir Abdullah ibn-Husein became king (May 25, 1946). It is the work of Professor Abdulkadir at-tannir. A text was supplied for it by Professor 'Abdulmún 'im ar-rifaa'i.

The national anthem of **Lebanon** is a regular strophic song of three stanzas. The words were written in Arabic by Lebanon's noted poet, Rachid Nakhlé. The first stanza may be transliterated in Roman letters as follows:

Koullouna lilouatann
Liloula lil a lam
Milou ay nizzaman
Sayfouna oual kalam
Sahlouna oualjabal
Manbi tonn lirrijal
Kaoulouna oual amal
Fi sabilil kamal.

There can be no satisfactory translation. A literal rendering would cover such trite patriotic stand-bys as everybody's eternal devotion to the homeland, its glory and its flag and the asseveration that every Lebanese will be a lion when trouble impends.

The musical setting is the work of Wadia Sabra, director of the Lebanese Conservatory of Music. It was the winning entry in a contest sponsored by the Lebanese parliament. It should be performed at a quick tempo in keeping with its tenor of military severity. The spirit it breathes is rather that of the French mandate than of Arab nationalism. The anthem was adopted officially by a Presidential decree of July 12, 1927.

In lieu of a national anthem, **Iraq** has a royal fanfare composed by Lieutenant A. Chaffon, a graduate of the Royal British Academy of Music and Conductor of the Iraqi "Music Band." It is played when the king enters and otherwise to mark solemn occasions.

According to another tradition, the composer of the fanfare was Major A. R. Murray. — The country acquired more recently a second anthem-like composition for which there is likewise no text. It is the work of the native Iraqi, Lewis Zambaka, who had studied music at Vienna. He composed his anthem equivalent after the Iraqi revolution of Juli 14, 1958. In this venture, he had the cooperation of Professor Uhl of the Music Academy of Vienna.

The royal fanfare sounds thus:

Zambaka's composition begins as follows:

141

Iran, the old Persian country, has a full-fledged anthem. The fanfare of Iraq does preserve a trace of Oriental music, especially in the third measure with the interval G-flat to A. Nothing of the sort can be said about the Iranian anthem. It is absolutely Western and was not even written in minor. The music is by Daud Nadjmi, the text by Mohamad Haschim Afsar. The anthem addresses itself to the Pahlawi dynasty. On official occasions, the "Song of Persia" is frequently sung but is not formally recognized as an anthem.

Egypt has a national march, "The Egyptian Royal Hymn." Legend has it that the composer was — Verdi. I should hasten to add that I have not been able to prove the legendary character of this amazing attribution. But there is no evidence in support of Verdi's authorship either. It is most likely that the Egyptian national march was posthumously attributed to Verdi on account of his enormous popularity in the country of the Nile.

This has its explanation in the fact that *Aida* was actually written for the opera house at Cairo where it was performed in 1871 as part of the celebration of the opening of the Suez Canal.

The march begins

It will be recalled that in 1958 Egypt and Syria joined forces announcing the formation of the **United Arab Republic.** Since 1961, when Syria withdrew from the union, the name United Arab Republic applies to Egypt alone. It has been kept alive because of President Nasser's hope that in the course of time other Arab states might accept his overall leadership. The song used as the national anthem of the United Arab Republic was originally meant as a war song for the Egyptian armed forces in the military operations of the Suez conflict (beginning November 1, 1956). The text was the work of the Egyptian journalist, Salah Shahien, whose friend, Kamal el Tawiel, contributed the music. The anthem was sung for the first time over the Egyptian radio by the popular singer of Arabic folk music, Miss Um Kulthum. In 1960, the song was officially declared the country's national anthem, for the old anthem of the Khedivs was no longer in use since King Faruk's abdication. The new anthem can hardly be called popular. The text is somewhat rhetorical:

> O thou, my weapon,
> In battle I longed to have thee nigh.
> Speak now and say: "Watchful am I;
> Where wert thou, war, all this time?"

As I am about to discuss the **Turkish** national anthem, I cannot help remembering an anecdote from my childhood. A Turkish dignitary had arrived in a little North Bohemian resort coming from Vienna. The local orchestra was ordered to welcome him with the Turkish national anthem, but the poor conductor could not remember anything about Turkey but the fact that it was a country with a half moon in its flag. So he wasted no time, and when the Turk entered he had his musicians greet him with the first movement of the Moonlight Sonata.

There is another anecdote, similar to the foregoing but relating to the naval review held by William II in 1895 on the occasion of the opening of the Kiel Canal. The Emperor was giving a great banquet on the flagship "Deutschland." Whenever a high dignitary came on board, the naval band had to play the national anthem of the country concerned. Things went along smoothly until a boat came along flying the red half-moon of Turkey. At that moment the bandleader found to his dismay that the music for the Turkish national anthem was not on hand. In this case the anecdote has it that the bandleader got out of the dilemma by having his band play the sentimental old song, "Friendly moon, thou movest gently" ["*Guter Mond, du gehst so stille*"]. The German locution, "*Einen Türken bauen*," which literally says "to build a Turk" but which signifies roughly "to put something across on someone," is said to have its origin in the ingenuity of this naval bandleader.

The old Turkey of the sultans got along with an instrumental march which the Egyptian Nedjib Pasha had compiled from various occidental patterns. Since the revolution it is often replaced by the "Mustapha Kemal March." However, an official Turkish national anthem known as the "Independence March," was adopted by the national assembly in 1921. The text, "*Korkma! Sönmez bu safa= klarda yüzen al sancak*," was written by Mehmed Akif. The music is by a composer named Zeki. It is in G minor in keeping with the character of Oriental music. But otherwise there is little about it that is Oriental. It does suggest Spanish or South American tango tunes.

Saudi Arabia has no national anthem in the strict sense of the term. It has instead a marching tune used to salute the king. The music was written by A. R. Al-Hatib. As originally published in 1950, it bore in Arabic the descriptive opening formula:

"In the name of God, the all-merciful, the anthem of salute to his majesty the king, who rests assured of all sacrificial devotion."

As one listens to this music, one cannot but think of a whole list of snippets from European tunes.

The tune of the national anthem of **Libya** is the work of the Egyptian composer Mohammed Abdul Wahab. The text was written by Al Bashir al Arebi. It goes back to 1952 and was sung with the functions of a national anthem in June, 1955, on the occasion of the second marriage of King Mohammed Idris I Senussi. The dotted notes of the tune give it a marchlike rhythm in which it is hard to discern elements of tribal or national folklore.

The refrain reads as follows:

> O my fatherland,
> Take my fighting force
> To defeat the enemies' cunning
> And connivance.
> Live! live forever!
> We are ready to die for you,
> O Libya!

A trace of Africanism may well be discerned in the **Tunisian** anthem which was chosen in 1958 on the basis of a contest in which 23 poets and 23 composers took part. The entries were submitted to various committees, the Tunisian president, and finally a people's assembly in Monastir, the birthplace of the president, where all the tunes were played one after the other. The successful entry, both in words and tune, reflects three basic moods: the struggle for freedom, love of peace, and the determination to fight for peace. The text begins:

> May our precious blood recall forevermore
> The nation's sacred struggle ...

The anthem of **Algeria** with its dotted rhythm has a fairly distinctive physiognomy. In this it stands on a par with the anthem of Morocco. The composer of the Algerian anthem is Mohammed Fawzi. The text, by the poet Moufdi Zakaria, was written on the eve of the execution of an Algerian nationalist. The text is French and begins:

> *Par les foudres qui anéantissent,*
> *Par les flots de sang et sans tache ...*

> (While the heavens rain destruction,
> Blameless and through floods of blood ...)

Morocco became an autonomous monarchy in 1956. Its national anthem has, strictly speaking, no text, for the words which originally went with the tune hark back to the times prior to the country's independence and are no longer in use. The music was composed by Leo Morgan.

Its minor character and dotted rhythm seem somehow more suggestive of Africa than holds true for most of the other African anthems.

The Islamic republic of **Mauritania** in West Africa, formerly a French colony, attained independence in 1958. The tune of its anthem was written by the orchestra conductor of the French radio, Nikiprovetzki, under the influence of a number of traditional songs of the native Mauritanian nomads *(Griots aux Morts)*. It would seem that this anthem, which has no text, is related to the Arabic maqams, particularly in its characteristic rhythm and the ground-bass repetition of a motif. It surely is one of the most original tunes of Africa.

The **Sudan** became an independent republic in 1956. That very same year, Sayed Ahmed Mohammed Saleh, member of the Supreme Council, wrote a text to which Lieutenant Ahmed Murgan contributed a tune intended to be used as a national anthem. It was officially recognized as such before the end of the year.

The text begins:

> We are the host of Allah, the host of the fatherland,
> When the caller calls for sacrifices, we shall not fail.

One of the most important African states is **Ethiopia.** The music of its national anthem was written in 1926 by an Armenian, Captain Kevork Nalbandian. The anthem was played for the first time on the occasion of the coronation of Emperor Haile Selassie I on November 2, 1930. The language of the text is Amharic. It has not been possible to ascertain the identity of the author. The opening lines read roughly:

> Blessed be O Ethiopia
> Through the force of God and of thy ruler.

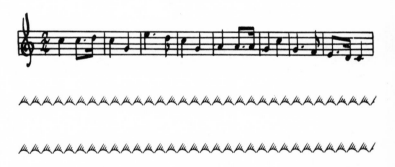

The national anthems which the numerous, newly established African states have adopted are on the whole — not unlike most of the Asian and South-American anthems — rather devoid of distinctive traits. They are often the work of European composers and rarely reflect traces of local folklore.

The African Negro Republic of **Liberia** has its own national anthem. The state was founded in 1821 as a home for emancipated slaves from North America and thus got its name, which is a somewhat unorthodox derivative from Latin *liber* 'free'. Its capital, Monrovia, was named after President Monroe of the United States (1816–1824). The text is by Daniel Bashiel Warner, third president of Liberia (1864 - 1868); the music is by Olmstead Luca who appears to have been born in the United States.

> All hail Liberia, hail.
> This glorious land of liberty
> Shall long be ours.
> Tho' new her name,
> Green be her fame,
> And mighty be her pow'rs.
> In joy and gladness with our hearts united
> We'll shout the freedom of a race benighted.
> Long live Liberia, happy land,
> A home of glorious liberty by God's command.

The tune cannot suggest Negro music in any way. There is no trace of Afro-American or straight African influence. The march= like beginning is much rather suggestive of a German student song. The trio recalls Viennese beergarden music and old-fashioned military marches. Toward the end there is even a dash of Mozart from the *Magic Flute*.

The British colony and protectorate of **Sierra Leone** on the west coast of Africa was granted independence in 1961. The original Portuguese form of the name was Sierra Leona. It is explained either as an allusion to the lion-like thunder in the hills or as reflecting a fancied resemblance of the mountains to the profile of a lion. The anthem of Sierra Leone was composed by its native son John Akar, Director of the Freetown radio. The tune is reminiscent of European folk songs. The text was written by C. Nelson Fyle.

The first lines of the text read:

High we exalt thee, realm of the free,
Great is the love we have for thee.

The **Republic of Guinea** on the west coast of Africa proclaimed its independence in 1958 under the name of French Guinea. Combining the old settlement of *Rivières du Sud* with the Futa Jallon tableland, it had formed, since 1904, a division of French West Africa. It uses as its national anthem a tune composed around 1880 by Fodeba Keita, subsequently Director of the African Ballet and Minister of the Interior of his country. There is no text accompanying the tune.

The former Senegambia of western Africa, which was a French possession, became an autonomous republic in 1958 and has been known as the republic of **Senegal** since 1960. The author of the text of the national anthem of Senegal is Leopold S. Senghor who became President of Senegal in 1960. The tune was composed by Herbert Peppert who also wrote the anthem of the Central African Republic.

The refrain of the anthem reads as follows:

Fibres de mon cœur vert, épaule contre épaule,
Mes plus-que frères, ô Sénégalais, debout!
Unissons la mer et les sources, unissons
La steppe et la forêt. Salut Afrique Mère.

(Fibers of my fresh heart, shoulder against shoulder,
My more than brothers, O Senegalese, arise!
Let us unite the ocean and the sources, let us unite
The steppe and the forest. Be saluted Mother Africa.)

The national anthem of the West African republic of **Mali** is based on an old war song. The territory of Mali comprises the region of the middle course of the Niger and the Upper Senegal. It traces its history to the twelfth century and the founding of the Empire of Mali by Soundiata Keita. The first president of the republic of Mali, Modibo Keita, belongs to the same family. The national anthem of Mali is the work of the French music teacher Gambetta. The melodic repetitions of the tune somehow make an originally African impression.

The text of the Mali anthem begins as follows:

A ton appel, Mali,
Pour ta prospérité,
Fidèles à ton destin,
Nous serons unis.

(At thy call, O Mali,
For thy prosperity,
Trustful of thy fate,
We stand as one.)

Among the territories named after the west African river Volta, **Upper Volta** is the most remarkable. It was part of the French colonial empire until 1958 when it achieved independence. Its anthem was written and composed by the Abbé Robert Quedraogo and is said to have been derived from autochthonous folk music. There is, by the way, a collection of folk songs of the region, which were brought together by a group of Catholic priests who then utilized them for liturgical purposes.

The text of the national anthem of Upper Volta begins:

Fière Volta de mes aïeux,
Ton soleil ardent et glorieux
Te revêt d'or et de clarté,
O Reine drappée de loyauté.

(Volta, you our fathers' delight,
Your glorious sun, burning and bright,
Robes you in brilliant hues of gold,
You, Queen, to whom in trust we hold.)

The tune seems to try to give evidence of its African origin through the repetition of a short motif.

The capital of the **Republic of Ivory Cost** is Abidjan, and its national anthem—which could not be the *"Marseillaise"*—is appropriately the *"Abidjanaise."* The country achieved independence in 1960, after having been under French rule from about 1883 on. It subsequently formed part of French West Africa. The text of the *"Abidjanaise"* was a team product. The music was contributed by the clergyman Pierre Michel Pango.

The first lines of the anthem read as follows:

> *Salut, ô terre d'espérance,*
> *Pays de l'hospitalité!*
> *Tes légions remplies de vaillance*
> *Ont relevé ta dignité.*

(Hail, land of hope and aspiration,
Thou home of hospitality.
Thy hosts, exempt from trepidation,
Have raised again thy dignity.)

The State of **Ghana** came into being in 1957, in succession to the British colony of the Gold Coast. It uses as its national anthem a tune composed for this purpose in 1956 by the Ghana-born composer Philip Gbeho. The composer also contributed the text which reads as follows:

> Hail the name of Ghana,
> Praise the heroes of our fight;

Raise in the sky the banner
Of freedom, hope, and might. —
Hail our nation's founder for whom we pray;
Cherish his faith from day to day;
Arise with joy, ye sons of Ghanaland;
And let Africa shine ever more.

♫♫♫♫♫♫♫♫♫♫♫♫♫♫♫♫♫♫♫♫♫♫♫♫♫♫♫♫♫

The formerly German protectorate of **Togo** became a mandate of the League of Nations in 1920 and of the United Nations in 1946. One part of it was administered by France, the rest by Britain. In 1947, the British part was incorporated in Ghana. The French part was granted independence in 1960. The Togo-born Alex Casimir Dosseh wrote both the melody and the text of the anthem of the new state. The tune is derived from a tom-tom song.

The text begins as follows:

> *Salut à toi de nos aïeux!*
> *Toi qui les rendais forts,*
> *Paisibles et joyeux . . .*

> (Greeted be in our father's name,
> You from whom their love of peace,
> Their strength and gladness came!)

♫♫♫♫♫♫♫♫♫♫♫♫♫♫♫♫♫♫♫♫♫♫♫♫♫♫♫♫♫

The west African republic of **Dahomey** is located on the coast of Guinea (the Slave Coast). Its history can be traced back to the seventeenth century when it formed part of the extensive kingdom of Allada. During the years from 1892 to 1894, the territory now known as Dahomey was subjected by the French. The country achieved independence in 1960 and has a national anthem of its own. The text was written by a group of young teachers, while the music was contributed by the clergyman G. Dagnon.

The opening lines of the text are as follows:

Enfants du Dahomey, debout!
La liberté d'un cri sonore
Chante aux premiers feux de l'aurore
Enfants du Dahomey, debout!

(Children of Dahomey, arise!
Hear the voice of freedom ringing,
By dawn's early fires singing:
Children of Dahomey, arise!)

Niger is a republic in central northern Africa which achieved independence in 1960. It must not be confused with Nigeria. The anthem of Niger is said to have been inspired by an old local hunters' tune. However, as one listens to the tune, one perceives nothing to suggest such an association. The anthem is not particularly African. Instead, it suggests the characteristics of French or German popular music. The title is *"La Nigérienne."* It was played officially for the first time in 1961 in Paris.

The anthem begins:

Auprès du grand Niger puissant
Qui rend la nature plus belle,

Soyons fiers et reconnaissants
De notre liberté nouvelle.

(By the majestic Niger's banks,
Which make nature's beauties still fairer,
Let us be proud and give our thanks,
Of a new freedom each the bearer.)

Nigeria, which lies on the Gulf of Guinea, shares with Niger only the fact that its name is derived from that of the Niger River. The territory now included in Nigeria was occupied by the British around 1880. It became an independent state in 1960. The text of the Nigerian anthem was written by the British subject Lilian Jean Williams. The music was composed by Francis Benda, likewise an Englishman (though the name Benda is of Czech origin). The anthem is without a physiognomy of its own. It begins as follows:

Nigeria, we hail thee,
Our own dear native land,
Though tribe and tongue may differ,
In brotherhood we stand.

Cameroon was a German protectorate from 1884 to 1918. In 1918 it was divided between the French and the British. In 1946 it became a mandate of the United Nations. The French sector became independent in 1960. A plebiscite was held in the British territory, with the result that the southern half of it joined the Republic of Cameroon, while the northern part fell to Nigeria. The national anthem of Cameroon is the work of students at the

Teachers' College of Foulassi. The text was written by Renée Jam Afam and the tune—strikingly reminiscent of the *Marseillaise*—by Samuel Minkyo Bamba.

The text of the anthem begins as follows:

> *O Cameroun, berceau de nos ancêtres,*
> *Autrefois tu vécus dans la barbarie.*
> *Comme un soleil tu commence à paraître,*
> *Peu à peu tu sors de ta sauvagerie.*

> (O Cameroon, cradle of our fathers,
> In days of yore thy state was barbary.
> Now like the sun, thy brightness ever gathers,
> And step by step thou conquer'st savagery.)

The **Republic of Chad** was formerly part of French Equatorial Africa. It was proclaimed an autonomous republic in 1958. It has an anthem written by two Catholic priests. The author of the words was Paul Villard, the composer Louis Jidrolle. Musically, the anthem of the Republic of Chad is hardly less undistinguished than numerous other anthems of the black continent.

The text begins:

> *Peuple Tschadien, debout et à l'ouvrage!*
> *Tu as conquis ta terre et ton droit!*

> (People of Chad, in righteous industry
> You hold possession of your land, your right!)

The **Central African Republic** was proclaimed on December 1, 1958, and granted autonomy as a member state of the French Community on August 13, 1960. The text of the anthem of the Republic was written by the Central African President, Barthélemy Boganda, who lost his life in an airplane accident in 1959. The music was written by the Frenchman Herbert Peppert. It is of interest to note that a considerable number of African anthems have tunes composed by Frenchmen.

Until 1960, when it achieved independence, **Gabon** was one of the four territories forming French Equatorial Africa. The population consists mainly of Bantu negroes and Pygmies. Most of the settlements are concentrated along the country's major river, the Ogowe. One such settlement is the missionary station of Lambaréné where Albert Schweitzer maintained his famous hospital. The national anthem of Gabon has the title, *"La Concorde"* ["Harmony"]. Both the text and the music are the work of Georges Damas. The anthem was chosen on the basis of a public contest. At the time when Damas wrote *"La Concorde,"* he was his country's ambassador in the Federal German Republic.

The beginning of the text reads as follows:

Uni dans la concorde et la fraternité,
Eveille-toi Gabon! Une Aurore se lève,
Encourage l'ardeur qui vibre et nous soulève.
C'est enfin notre essor vers la felicité.

(In harmony at one, in brotherhood we stand,
Awake Gabon, awake! Behold, the day is breaking,
That our hearts anew in vibrant pride be waking.
The soaring flight is on, the hour of bliss at hand.)

At the instigation of the **Congolese** journalist Georges Kimbanqui, the text and the tune of the song, *"La Congolaise,"* were written by Jean Royer, Joseph Spadilière, and Jacques Tondra. The national assembly, in secret session, endorsed the anthem overwhelmingly, and on November 4, 1959, "La Congolaise" officially became the national anthem of the Republic of Congo, the former French Middle Congo, of which Brazzaville is the capital.

The national anthem of the Republic of The Congo, the former Belgian Congo, of which Léopoldville is the capital was written in Louvain at the instigation of a group of Congolese students. Words and music are the work of the Jesuit Father S. Boka and the student J. Lutumba.

The anthem of the Republic of Congo begins:

The anthem of the Republic of The Congo begins:

North and west of Lake Victoria in East Africa lies the former British protectorate of **Uganda** which became independent in 1962. The national anthem of Uganda was composed by G. Kakoma, a music teacher attached to the Ministry of Education of Kabaka. The text of the anthem was worked out by Kakoma in cooperation with P. Wingard, a teacher of English at Makerere College. The anthem was performed for the first time in August, 1962, and broadcast at the time by all radio stations of the country.

The first two lines of the text read:

> O Uganda! May God uphold thee!
> We lay our future in thy hand.

In the formerly British-occupied territory of **Kenya** in East Africa, there were Arabic trading posts as far back as the tenth century. The turbulent history of the country, in which Portuguese, British, German and Zanzibari intervention played a role, reached its climax in 1963 when the country achieved independence. The national anthem of Kenya is based on a traditional African folksong and resulted from the cooperative efforts of a committee of five musicians.

The text was produced by the same committee. It begins as follows:

> O God of all creation,
> Bless this our land and nation.
> Justice be our shield and defender;
> May we dwell in unity,
> Peace and liberty;
> Plenty be found within our borders.

Somalia constituted itself an independent republic in 1960. Its territory had been held in part by the French, in part by the British, and in part by the Italians. It also includes the former British Somaliland. Its anthem, which has no text, was written by the Italian composer Giuseppe Blanc from Turin.

The Belgian mandate of **Ruanda-Urundi** in Central Africa became independent in 1962. Its national anthem was written by Michael Habarurema. The dotted notes of this anthem give it the character of a march.

The first two lines read:

> *Rwanda, oh ma patrie, toi honneur et victoire,*
> *Quand je considère tes merveilles, je me plais à chanter.*

(Ruanda, o my country, your honor and victory,
When I consider your marvels, I cannot but wish to sing.)

Burundi re-achieved independence on July 1, 1961, and was given forthwith a national anthem with a text by the African clergyman Jean-Baptiste Ntabokaja and a tune by the clergyman Marc Barengayabo. The country is again a kingdom, and it is noteworthy that its anthem mentions the name of the old God Imana. The royal dynasty can be traced back to about 1500. Its establishment is still commemorated in a national celebration known as the "Umuganuro." The following is the beginning of the tune of its anthem:

The text begins:

> *Cher Burundi, ô doux pays,*
> *Prends place dans le concert des nations,*
> *En tout bien tout honneur accède à l'indépendance.*

(Dear Burundi, o sweet land,
Take thy place in the concert of nations,
In high weal, high honor, attain thy independence.)

The **Republic of Tanzania** came into being in 1964 when the Republic of Tanganyika merged with Zanzibar. The former sultanate of Zanzibar had achieved independence in 1963 and was a republic since January, 1964. Tanganyika achieved self-government in 1961, having been a United Nations' trust territory under British administration from 1946. The national anthem of Tanzania is that of Tanganyika. It is the work of the South-African composer Enoch Sontonga who was connected with the Christian Mission. The anthem was performed for the first time by the police band of Dar-es-Salaam on December 9, 1961, as part of the ceremonies of the declaration of independence of Tanganyika.

The text of the national anthem of Tanzania begins:

> God bless Tanganyika,
> Grant eternal freedom and unity
> To its sons and daughters.
> God bless Tanganyika and its people.

The former British protectorate of Nyasaland achieved independence in 1964 as the republic of **Malawi**. Its national anthem is the work of its native son, Michael Fred P. Sauka.

The text of the anthem begins:

> O God, bless our land of Malawi,
> Keep it a land of peace.

The independent **Malagasy** republic was proclaimed on June 26, 1960. It occupies the island of Madagascar, the fourth largest island in the world, in the Indian Ocean off the southeast coast of Africa. The first Europeans to visit Madagascar were the Portuguese in 1506. In the early nineteenth century, the Hòva tribe extended its rule over a large part of the island. The British began to occupy Madagascar from 1842 to 1846, but in 1885 France confirmed her claim to it as a French protectorate. In 1897, the island ceased to be a kingdom. The present republic has a national anthem composed by Norbert Rabarsoa, a native of Tananarive. The text is by the English pastor Rabajaso. The dotted notes of the tune make it sound somewhat like a central-European march.

The text of the Malagasy anthem begins:

> *O bien-aimée terre de nos ancêtres!*
> *Nous voulons mettre à ton service*
> *Notre être, notre cœur et notre âme,*
> *Ce que nous avons de plus précieux et de plus digne.*

> (O thou, beloved land of our fathers!
> Ready we stand to give into your service

All that we are, with heart and soul,
All that we have most precious and most worthy.)

The national anthem of the **Union of South Africa** bears the title, *"Die Stem van Suid Afrika"* ("The Voice of South Africa"). It was written in 1918 by C. J. Langenhoven, a writer known for his efforts to promote Afrikaans as a literary language distinct from Dutch. The tune that goes with Langenhoven's text was composed by M. L. de Villiers, an organist and choral composer well known throughout South Africa. *"Die Stem van Suid Afrika"* was sung for the first time in public in 1928. On the occasion of the opening of Parliament on February 11, 1938, Prime Minister Hertzog announced that he had decided to have the *"Stem"* played on a par with the British anthem, "God Save the King," and in 1952 Minister President Malan released an English version that was to be regarded as the official translation. In 1958, *"Die Stem"* was declared the official national anthem, with the understanding that it was no longer obligatory to play the British anthem on state occasions.

The first stanza of the English version of *"Die Stem"* reads as follows:

Ringing out from our blue heavens, from our deep seas breaking
round;
Over granite-rooted mountains where the echoing crags resound;
From our plains where creaking wagons etched their trails into the
earth —
Calls the spirit of our Country, of the land that gave us birth.
Loudly peals the answering chorus: We are thine, and we shall
stand,
Be it life or death, to answer when you call, beloved land.

The former Orange Free State used to sing and still sings the song *"Heft Burgers 't lied de vrijheid an"* ("Let's sing the song of liberty").

The former Transvaal still cherishes its song, *"Kent gij dat volk vol heldenmoed"* ("Know ye this race of bravery"), which was written and set to music (1875) by Cathrine Felicie van Rees who is more generally known for her operettas.

THE ORIENT

The countries of the Orient have been slow in taking up contact with the Western World although their cultures form in more senses than one the ultimate bases of Occidental civilization. The principle of national anthems — the idea that a song can inspire the multitudes with patriotic and if need be bellicose fervor — was a slow growth in Europe too, and all other countries of the world have merely imitated it in course of time.

Let us speak first of the Middle Empire of **China.** It did have from early times a series of temple anthems whose archaic tone patterns have in some instances been kept alive into modern times. But these have little or nothing to do with national anthems in the contemporary sense. The first full-fledged national anthem of China was originally the party song of the Kuomintang. When this group took over the government, their song became an official Chinese national song. The words were by Dr. Sun Yat-Sen (1867 to 1925) and were taken from a speech which this poet, philosopher, and politician had addressed to the students of the Whampoa Mi= litary Academy.

The opening words, "San Min Chu I," signify the three princip= les of the people. This is a reference to Dr. Sun's political philo= sophy which he had formulated as early as 1898 in terms of the three basic ideals of nationalism, democracy, and socialism. Sun's revolutionary aims, from 1905 on, were consciously interpreted as the implementation of the three principles in all spheres of government and administration.

The music is by Ch'eng Mao-Yün and was the winning entry in a public competition held by the Kuomintang.

The tune is simple and keeps the balance between Western melodics and the native pentatonic system without half tones. It runs as follows:

Through the vicissitudes of history the Chinese national anthem has come to be, restrictedly, the anthem of the Republic of China (i e., Nationalist China) on Taiwan. Communist **China** (i. e., mainland China) has its own anthem, the "Chung-Ha-Jen-Min Gung-Ho Guo," which appears to be more aggressive in character than its Taiwan counterpart.

The anthem of mainland China has an interesting history. The text was written in 1932, after the Japanese invasion of Manchuria, by the dramatist T'ien Han. The music was contributed by Nie Erh, a composer who subsequently died in Japanese exile. The song was originally a call to arms in the fight against the Japanese. Although it had the endorsement of the government of Chiang Kai-Shek, the song remained popular with the Communists until in 1949 it was finally adopted as the official national anthem of China. The tune of this "March of the Volunteers" is thoroughly Occidental and thus in keeping with the Marxist ideal of contemporary Communist China. It features dotted notes, imparting to it a marching rhythm that symbolizes Marxist thought, and hence contrasts sharply with the anthem of Nationalist China.

The message of the opening lines may be stated as follows:

Arise! We are no longer ready to be slaves!
Build the Great Wall anew from flesh and blood!
The people of China faces extreme danger.
Irate cries issue forth from the oppressed.

The **Japanese** national anthem, "*Kimi-ga-yo*" (The Emperor's House"), embodies material drawn from old sources which go back as far as the ninth century. It was composed by Hayashi Hironokami in 1880 and revised by Franz Eckert who was born in Silesia, Germany, in 1852 and died at Seoul, Korea, in 1916. It begins:

Here again we find a pentatonic pattern. But while the Chinese use no half tones, the Japanese do. The Japanese anthem, however, shows the influence of Chinese folk ways.

The **Philippines** have a national anthem which evolved from a patriotic march by the professional composer and musician Julian Felipe. It was written in 1898 at the request of General Emilio Aguinaldo, Filipino leader in the rebellion against Spain during the years from 1896 to 1898. It embodies some striking reminis= cences of the old order as represented by the Spanish Royal March and again—in what came to be the C-major refrain of the anthem— it suggests a strong influence of the *Marseillaise*. But these de= pendencies do not lessen the appeal of its forceful and spirited pace.

Under the title of "*Marcha Nacional Filipina*" ("Filipino National March"), it was performed for the first time in conjunction with the reading of the Act of Proclamation of Philippine Independence on June 12, 1898. It is interesting to note that Commodore Dewey, Commander of the American Squadron anchored at the port of Cavite, was so impressed with the tune that he requested several copies of it which he forwarded to the United States. Yet after the establishment of American sovereignty in the Philippines the per= formance of the March was discouraged, not to say forbidden. It had meanwhile attained the status of a national song through the poem written for it by the young patriot José Palma in Bautista, Pangasinan, in August, 1899. Under the title of *"Filipinas"* this poem was first published on September 3, 1899, in the newspaper *La Independencia*. The first of its two stanzas reads in the original Spanish:

> *Tierra adorada,*
> *Hija del Sol de Oriente,*
> *Su fuego ardiente*
> *En tí latiendo está.*
> *Patria de Amores,*
> *Del heroismo cuna,*
> *Los invasores*
> *No te hollaran jamás.*
> *Tierra de dichas, de sol y amores,*
> *En tu regazo dulce es vivir,*
> *Es una gloria para tus hijos,*
> *Cuando te ofenden, por tí morir.*

In course of time American opposition to the song relaxed to the point of permitting the public performance of the anthem on condition that it be followed by the "Star-Spangled Banner." Under American rule various English translations were made, the most successful being that by Camilo Osias:

> Land of the morning,
> Child of the sun returning,
> With fervor burning
> Thee do our souls adore.
> Land dear and holy,
> Cradle of noble heroes,
> Ne'er shall invaders
> Trample thy sacred shore.
> Beautiful land of love, O land of light,
> In thine embrace 'tis rapture to lie.
> But it is glory ever, when thou art wronged,
> For us thy sons, to suffer and die.

It goes without saying that the national anthem of the Philippines has also been translated into Tagalog, the language of one of the most numerous native peoples of the Philippines. The Tagalog version has gained in popularity since 1946 when the Philippines achieved independence from the United States.

The division of **Korea** into a Communist People's Republic in the North and an independent Democratic Republic in the South is reflected in the existence of two Korean national anthems. The annexation of Korea or Chosen by the Japanese goes back to 1910. What is now the North Korean anthem was written in 1946 during the struggle for a unified state. The text is by Pak Se Jen and the music by Kim Won Gûn. The song was given official recognition after the proclamation of the People's Republic in 1949.

During the Japanese rule, the southern part of the country grew fond of a song which, though initially sung exclusively in more or less private circles, rose to a status of official recognition after the defeat of the Japanese. The well-known composer An Ik Tae, who had studied music in Germany, is responsible for the arrangement currently in use. A comparison of the two anthems yields no striking conclusions, except possibly for the fact that the northern anthem is vaguely reminiscent of the Soviet anthem.

The Northern anthem begins roughly:

Morning sun, shine over the rivers and mountains,
Over the three thousand mile expanse of our beautiful country
Which is rich in natural resources,
And over the splendor of its people.

The Southern anthem begins as follows:

Until the eastern sea dries out,
Until Mount Paek Tu is leveled,
God will safeguard this land of ours.

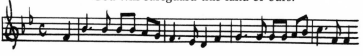

Afghanistan adopted a national anthem in 1930. It is played by military bands on all official occasions and is being taught in the schools. The tune is by Mohamed Faruk, the Persian text by Mohammed Makhtar. The opening lines read approximately:

Our brave and much-beloved ruler,
Loyally we stand behind thee . . .

And the refrain confirms in the character of a fanfare:

O our ever-loving king.

The Republic of **Pakistan** on the subcontinent of India has two official languages, Urdu and Bengali. The population of Pakistan is almost entirely Mohammedan. It belongs to the British Commonwealth of Nations. The state of Pakistan in its present form was established in 1947. The political and religious differences between India and Pakistan, which are linked by a relationship of latent hostility, are reflected in the contrasting tunes and texts of their national anthems. In fact, the Pakistani anthem with its dotted European marching rhythm is quite aggressive, and the notorious determination of an Islamic state is additionally made vocal in the words of the text. The tune was composed by Ahmad C. Chagla. The text is in Urdu and was written by Abul Asar Hafis Jullundri.

The meaning of the opening lines of the text is reflected in the following:

> Blessed be, thou sacred country,
> Blissful thy beautiful lands.
> Thou symbol of determination,
> O Pakistan,
> Blessed be, thou stronghold of faith.

The song, *"Janaganamana"* by Rabindranath Tagore (1861–1941), was sung for the first time in 1911 at a meeting of the **Indian** Congress in Calcutta. The language is Hindi with interspersed Sanskrit words. Mahatma Ghandi referred to it as a devotional hymn, while the poet himself, who translated it into English in 1919, called it the morning song of India. Outside of India, the first official performance of the song occurred in 1947 in the General Assembly of the United Nations.

The music of *"Janaganamana,"* likewise by Rabindranath Tagore, was arranged for military bands by two Englishmen, Herbert Murrill and Norman Richardson. This arrangement was officially approved by the government of India.

Another song, *"Vande Mataram,"* by Bankim Chandra Chaterjee (1838–1894), appeared in print in 1882 in the author's novel *"Ananda Math."* This song played an important part during the Indian struggle for freedom. Its first public performance occurred at a session of the Indian National Congress in 1896. The music was contributed by Rabindranath Tagore, and in course of time the first two words of the song became a slogan of the nationalist movement.

In 1950, it was decreed that Rabindranath Tagore's *"Janaganamana"* should alone be recognized as the Indian national anthem, while the *"Vande Mataram"* was permitted to be used on a par with it.

It is difficult to decide whether the tune of the official Indian anthem does indeed, as has been suggested, reflect the old Indian ragas. The first measures are almost reminiscent of the Slovac national anthem but represent in fact neither more nor less than an ascending and descending tetrachord.

The uniformity of the rhythm is remarkable too.

Ceylon, known to the ancients as Taprobane, was — from the sixteenth century on — a bone of contention between the Portuguese, the Dutch, and the British. In 1948, Ceylon became a dominion in the British Commonwealth. The song currently in use as the national anthem of Ceylon was written in Singhalese by Ananda Samarakoon. Though not written for the purpose, it was revived and submitted as an entry in a public contest for the selection of the national anthem. Since the individual stanzas and the corresponding music are very long, it is customary on official occasions to play only the first six measures.

The opening lines of the text run somewhat as follows:

> I bow to thee, Mother,
> Blessed Lanka.
> I bow to thee, I bow to thee, Mother.

The earliest population of what is now **Laos** were the australoasiatic Kha. These were superseded by the Khmer. In 1356, the great kingdom of Luang-Prabang was established which in course of time split up in several parts. These were conquered by Siam and became a French protectorate in 1893. From 1949 to 1954 Laos was an independent state within the French Union. It was admitted to the United Nations in 1955. During the Indo-China war the communists in the north established the opposition government of the Pathet Lao. The country has a national anthem written by S. E. Thondy (one-time member of the cabinet with the two portfolios of postal affairs and fine arts). Despite the prevailing chaotic conditions, the anthem has managed to win popular acceptance. The dotted quavers as well as some other characteristics of the tune are reminiscent of the anthem of South Vietnam.

The text begins:

Of high fame was of yore throughout Asia the race of Lao.
It was when the people of Lao was one in love.

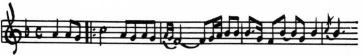

The former East Indian kingdom of **Cambodia** comprised the basin of the lower Mekong River exclusive of the delta. The country has an interesting and varied history. This goes back to the sixth century when the Khmer conquered the empire of Funam established in Farther India by invaders from India proper. The area was made a French protectorate in 1867 and overrun by the Japanese during the Second World War. Subsequently it was part of the French Union and achieved independence in 1955.

The text of the national anthem of Cambodia was written by Chuon Nath, head of a Buddhist order. The tune was contributed by F. Perrucher and J. Jekyll. The language of the text is Khmer. The song was officially recognized as the national anthem of Cambodia in 1941. The tune manifests considerable originality. It is to be sung with hymnic solemnity and appears to reflect older models.

The first stanza reads in translation:

> May the heavens protect our king
> And grant him happiness and fame,
> So that he be our ruler,
> He, son of great generations,
> Lord of the proud realm of old.

Vietnam, the Annamese country of the south, is split — like Korea — into a northern communist and a southern democratic part. With the defeat of the Japanese and the end of the Second World War, the country was reoccupied by the French who had previously held it for a long time. However, the French rule could not be maintained; the ensuing bloody conflict between France and Vietnam was settled at the Geneva Conference of 1954.

A comparison of the anthems of the two Vietnams reveals a relationship similar to that between the anthems of the two Chinas. The anthem of North Vietnam was written in 1944 by Van-Cao and given official standing in 1956. The anthem of South Vietnam is the work of a student named Luu-Huu-Phuoc. The texts of the two anthems are quite comparable except that that of North Vietnam appears to be the more aggressive. The anthem of South Vietnam, written in 1943, received official recognition in 1948.

The following is an illustration of the North Vietnamese anthem. It is followed by a similar illustration for South Vietnam.

The northern text begins:

> Inspired by the thought of saving the country
> The Vietnamese army marches on.

The anthem sung in the south begins:

> Youth of Vietnam, arise, the fatherland calls you.
> Onward we march, in unity blazing our trail.

The present **Burma,** styled the Union of Burma, became an independent republic in 1948. It had been occupied by the Japanese in 1942. For more than a century prior to that event it had been under British rule, being administered as a province of British India from 1886 to 1937. The anthem of Burma is by Th Kin Ba Thoung. It was sung as early as 1928 as a political song.

The text begins:

> May never in your hearts the world take Burma's place,
> The gift of ages given us to love and grace.
> To Burma's unity belong our lives.

In the thirteenth century, the Lao-Tai, a people of paleo-mongolian race established the kingdom of Sukhotai in what is now **Thailand,** the "Land of the Free," in Farther India. The Lao-Tai mingled with the Khmer. The modern Siamese or Thai are their joint descendants. Throughout the centuries the territory of Thailand was the theater of many wars involving the Burmese and the Chinese. In 1782 Phaya Chakkri founded the dynasty that is still ruling today. In 1932, the previously absolute rule was replaced by a constitutional monarchy. In the Second World War Thailand sided with the Japanese. In 1946 the country was admitted to the United Nations.

The national anthem of Thailand dates from 1932. The music was written by Phra Chen Duriyanga, the text by Khun Vichit Madrah. Before 1932, a regal hymn filled some of the functions of a national anthem. It was played exclusively when the king or the queen appeared in person. The composer of the regal hymn was reportedly an Englishmen. An arrangement of the tune is ascribed to a German by the name of Veit. This Veit is the father

of the composer of the national anthem currently in use. The
text currently in use with the tune of the former regal hymn was
written by King Rama VI.

This short illustration suffices to show the march-like, European character of the tune of the' anthem of Thailand. The text
begins as follows:

> Thailand is the embodiment of all the blood,
> Of all the flesh of Thailand's race.
> Thailand to the Tai ...

Malaysia is a federation of 14 states established in 1963. It includes — in addition to the 11 states previously affiliated in the
Federation of Malaya — the states of Singapore, Sarawak, and
Sabah (formerly British North Borneo). The national anthem of
Malaysia is that of the old Federation of Malaya. All the member
states of Malaysia, with the exception of Penang and Malacca,
have their own anthem apart from that of the Federation.

The history of the Malaysian national anthem goes back to the
year 1901 and the coronation of King Edward VII in London.
Among the dignitaries attending the celebration was the ruler of
Perak (which was and is one of the Malay States). He was greeted
with the tune of a song of the people of his country which his
secretary had whistled to the orchestra leader. This tune, with a
text written for it by Raja Musa Ibni Almarhum Abdul Aziz, came
to be the anthem of Perak. When Perak became part of the Federation of Malaya, its anthem became that of the Federation
which, as stated before, was subsequently taken over by Malaysia.

The beginning of the text of the Malaysian anthem reads approximately:

> O thou homeland!
> Thy people, watchful and united, jubilates ...

𝄢𝄞 (rhythmic notation)

The area known today as **Indonesia** appears to have received its first settlers from East India. Its history reveals a variety of cultural strata. The Dutch influence dates from 1602 when the Netherlands East India Company began its career of acquiring vast areas of the island empire and the adjacent continent. In 1941, all of Netherlands India was occupied by the Japanese. The Japanese tolerated the nationalist movement the beginnings of which go very far back. The final outcome of this development was the proclamation in 1945 of an independent Indonesian republic. The text of what is now the national anthem of Indonesia was recited as early as 1928 by its author, Supratman, with inspiring effect on the audience. The tune was likewise composed by Supratman. There is in it no trace of the age-old Indonesian musical culture. Instead it reflects the tradition of European march music.

The opening lines of the text read:

> Indonesia, fatherland,
> You my homeland.
> Here I stand
> To serve you, kindly mother.

LATIN AMERICA

As one considers the South American national anthems in general one is struck by the fact that in comparison with European and North American anthems they are extremely elaborate, even pretentious, and certainly not folklike. They all depend to a higher or lesser degree on models drawn from the Italian opera of the first half of the nineteenth century. In most cases these anthems have noisy preludes and repeated interludes with kettledrums and trumpets. Throughout they testify to the South American pre= dilection for fancy and pomp, for parades and processions. Whoever has seen a Corpus-Christi or Easter procession in Southern Spain will sense their connection with these marching hymns of South America. Still, they are in no way related to autochthonous Spanish or Portuguese music and even less to the music of the Indian natives.

In his book, *Music of Latin America*, Nicolas Slonimsky reports that native Latin-American musicians regard their national anthems as part of their peoples' lore. This attitude can only be justified because the anthems — often written by Italian and some= times by German-born musicians — do reflect the emotional and intellectual tenor of the population.

In addition to a considerable treasure of folk music the **Argen-tine Republic** can also boast a sort of official music. An example of the latter type is the *"Marcha de la Patria"* ("March of the Fatherland"), the official national anthem of Argentina which was carried to Peru and Chile by Argentine soldiers in the army of General San Martín, the liberator of those two countries. There is an account of how the general in 1818 during a great celebration at Santiago de Chile magnetized the crowd by singing the Argentine anthem with his tremendous basso voice. Similar examples of "official" music are the *"Canción Patriotica"* by Esteban de Lucca, the *"Himno de los Restauradores"* by Rivera Indarte, and the *"Marcha Triunfal"* by Artigas.

The *"Marcha de la Patria"* was written by Vicente Lopez y Planes and set to music by Blas Parera in 1813. Amongst all anthems it is the longest composition — just as the Greek anthem has the distinction of having the largest number of stanzas. The composer, Blas Parera, was a music teacher, and it seems that he was equally inspired by his familiarity with the Italian operas of Rossini and Donizetti and by his admiration for the German composers of sonatas like Haydn and Mozart. The anthem prelude consists of two parts. The first is classical in style, the second with its triplets of eighths recalls the Italian opera. The anthem proper is very dignified, and the refrain, introduced by an instrumental interlude, is convincing and powerful. It was declared the official Argentine national anthem by a resolution

of the *Asemblea General* on May 11, 1813. On March 30, 1900, a government decree required it to be performed at all public functions as well as in the schools and institutions of higher learning throughout the country.

The **Bolivian** anthem is somewhat less elaborate but it rep=
resents essentially the same type as that of Argentina. The words
are by Ignacio de Sanjines (1786—1864), the music by the Italian
L. Benedetto Vincenti. Sanjines was a lawyer and scholar of high
standing and a fervent patriot. He was among the signers of his
country's declaration of independence and its first constitution.

The music is a vocal specimen in the heroic style of the Italian
opera. Its rhythm with dotted quavers, which can inspire the Boliv=
ians with patriotic enthusiasm, has very little to do with native
Indian music or again with the work of those musicians who drew
on the treasures of Bolivian folklore as for instance Caba, Bravo,
Roncal, Vargas, and others.

The text of the anthem begins:

> *Bolivianos: el hado propicio*
> *Coronó nuestros votos y anhelo* . . .

> (Bolivians: a provident destiny
> Has fulfilled our vows and endeavor . . .)

The music of the original **Brazilian** anthem was written by
Don Pedro I. We have mentioned this fact in connection with the
Portuguese anthem. Pedro was quite an amateur musician. He
actually wrote a complete opera, and the overture of it was per=
formed in Paris in 1832. His anthem — that is, the first Brazilian
anthem which survived as the anthem of Portugal — is said to have
been written by him on September 7, 1822 between 5.30 and

9 P. M., and that same night,— tradition has it — he sang it in São Paolo accompanied by a chorus.

After Pedro's abdication in 1831, a new anthem was called for. The music was written by Francisco Manoel da Silva (1795–1865), court composer to Pedro II and founder of the National Con= servatory and the Philharmonic Orchestra in Rio de Janeiro.

This anthem has again an introduction with dotted quavers partly in "lombard rhythms" whose somewhat pretentious elegance is directly suggestive of Rossini's *Barber of Seville.* The first phrase,

however, occurs in a very popular Hungarian Czardas. Except for some rather conventional passages, the Brazilian anthem is digni= fied and expressive of patriotic devotion.

The text of the anthem alluded to the political events of the year 1831 and was soon felt to be somewhat inappropriate. When Brazil became a republic in 1889, a public contest was instituted for the purpose of selecting a brand new anthem. The winning entry was a composition by Leopoldo Miguez with words by Medeiros e Albuquerque, but when it was compared with the traditional anthem, a compromise seemed advisable whereby Manoel's work was kept as the national anthem and that of Miguez was adopted as the anthem of the republic. In 1922 a new text was officially adopted for Manoel's anthem. It is by Osorio Duque Estrada (1870–1927) and breathes a spirit of fervent patriotism free from allusions to transitory phases of the country's history.

The **Chilean** anthem had originally a text written by the patriot
Bernardo de Vera y Pintado (1780—1827). It sang in great detail
the praises of the revolution of September 18, 1810. In 1847 a
new peace treaty was signed between the Republic of Chile and
Spain, and at this time Senhor Eusebio Lillo, a journalist and well-
known poet, was commissioned to write a new anthem with more
restrained sentiments in regard to the old mother country. The
music of the anthem is by Ramón Carnicer (1789—1855). It was
written in 1828. According to Nicolas Slonimsky, the composer
never set foot on Chilean soil.

The beginning of the anthem runs as follows:

When one places this passage next to the first measures of the
Bolivian anthem, one is confronted with one more illustration of
the fact that most South American anthems breathe about the
same spirit. The Chilean tune is of course likewise introduced by
a noisy prelude which, together with the militant vigor of the
anthem itself, represents a fine specimen of South American
musical nationalism.

> *Ha cesado la lucha sangrienta,*
> *Ya es hermano el que ayer opresor ...*
>
> (Has ceased now the battle so bloody,
> We call brethren the oppressors of yore ...)

The music of the national anthem of **Colombia** was written by
the Italian tenor Orestes Sindici who had arrived in Bogotá with

an Italian opera company and for some reason decided to stay on. His remains rest in a cemetery at Bogotá. The lines of the anthem are by Rafael Núñez (1825–1894), the great statesman who served his country as president for no less than four terms (between 1880 and 1888). The Italian inspiration of the music is quite apparent. There is a triumphant prelude followed by the tune

with the words

¡Oh, gloria inmarcesible!
¡Oh júbilo inmortal!
En surcos de dolores
El bien germina ya.

(O glory that cannot wither!
Delight that cannot die!
In furrows drawn by anguish
The good already sprouts.)

There is an amusing story about the national anthem of **Costa Rica** for which we are likewise indebted to Nicolas Slonimsky. When in 1853 the plenipotentiaries of Great Britain and the United States arrived in San José, the capital of Costa Rica, the president of the republic decided that the two gentlemen should be wel= comed to the strains of the national anthem. The trouble was that Costa Rica had no national anthem. To remove this slight obstacle, Manuel María Gutiérrez (1829–1887), who enjoyed the reputation of being his country's foremost practicing musician, was ordered to compose one. The poor devil insisted that he knew nothing about the art of musical composition. But that did him no good. He was thrown into prison and promised that he would not be re= leased until he had produced a usable piece of music. The resulting composition was first performed in the National Assembly of San José on June 11, 1853. The story may be apocryphal, for there are sources which give the date of the anthem as 1821. However that be, with its text by José Maria Zeledón (officially adopted in 1900 as the result of a public contest), the anthem of Costa Rica is a very respectable composition. It is somewhat conventional and suggests vaguely the style of contemporary German glee club arrangements.

> *Noble patria, tu hermosa bandera*
> *Expresión de tu vida nos da ...*

> (Noble country, thy beautiful banner
> Is for us a symbol of thy life ...)

Next to the Costa Rican anthem we may place the opening measures of that of **Cuba**.

The rhythmic and melodic similarity of the two is striking indeed. The Cuban text begins:

> *Al combate corred, bayameses,*
> *Que la patria os contempla orgullosa ...*

> (To the fray, o men of Bayamo,
> The country look upon you with pride ...)

In keeping with its first line, the anthem is also known as the *"Himno de Bayamo."* The author (poet and composer) is Pedro Figueredo (1819–1870). He played a distinguished part in the movement of the Cuban patriots against the Spanish oppressors and commanded the revolutionary forces in the battle of Bayamo in October, 1868. When in the course of this operation the village of Guanabacoa was stormed, he felt the inspiration to write both the words and the tune of the anthem. In 1870 he was taken pris= oner by the Spaniards. He was condemned to death and executed.

The *"Himno Nacional de la República Dominicana"* was com= posed by José Reyes (1835–1905). It was preceded by the *"Himno de la Independencia"* by Juan Bautista Alfonseca, the first com= poser to use the folk music of the **Dominican Republic** in his works.

The text of the Reyes anthem is by Emilio Prud'homme and begins as follows with an allusion to the native name of the island of Santo Domingo:

> *Quisqueyanos valientes, alcemos*
> *Nuestro canto con viva emoción . . .*

> (Brave men of Quisqueya, let's raise our voices
> To sing our song with heartfelt emotion . . .)

The triumphal marchlike melody, again reminiscent of nine= teenth century Italian opera, has also a touch of the *Marseillaise.* The music begins as follows:

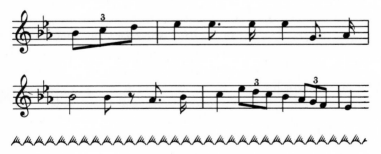

The composer of the anthem of **Ecuador** was Antonio Neumane or Neumann, born of German parents in Quito in 1818. He died there in 1871. He was also the first director of the National Conservatory in Quito which was established in 1870. The author of the text was Juan León Mera (1832—1894), a scholar and journalist. In his later years he was the President of the Senate of Ecuador. The anthem had been in use for a considerable length of time before it was officially recognized in 1886 by a government decree.

> *¡Salve, oh Patria, mil veces! ¡Oh Patria,*
> *Gloria a tí! Ya tu pecho rebosa*
> *Gozo y paz, y tu frente radiosa*
> *Más que el sol contemplamos lucir.*

(Hail, o my country, a thousand times hail!
Glory to thee while thy heart overflows
With joy and with peace, and thy radiant forehead
Shines to our eyes more brightly than the sun.)

The introduction to this anthem of marchlike rhythm is written in the grandiloquent style one is apt to associate with romantic piano sonatas. The tune is replete with dash and ardor and admits no doubt in regard to the German background of the composer.

The anthem of **El Salvador** has a text written by Juan J. Cañas. It was composed by one Juan Aberle whose German name squares poorly with the claim that he hailed from Italy. He settled in El Salvador in 1845 and became the teacher of a whole generation of musicians of his new country as also of Guatemala. Slonimsky reports that the government of Guatemala had a gold medal struck for him with the inscription, "To the Prince of Central American Music." His own teacher was José Escolástico Andrino.

The first lines of the anthem read:

Saludemos la patria orgullosos
De hijos suyos podernos llamar ...

(O let's salute our country, our hearts full of pride
That its children ourselves we may call...)

The beginning of the music is marked by a solemn flourish of trumpets which recurs throughout this marchlike composition. The trio is a striking reminiscence of the "Coronation March" in Meyerbeer's *Prophet.*

The anthem of **Guatemala** goes back to 1887 and was the winning entry in a public competition. The lines are by José Joaquín Palma (1844–1911), the tune by Rafael Alvarez.

¡Guatemala feliz! Que tus aras
No profane jamás el verdugo ...

(Guatemala blessed! May thy altars
Never be profaned by the lash ...)

After a prelude of fanfares the march proper begins as follows:

In contrast to almost all the other South American anthems, that of **Haiti** — though typically South American — shares certain characteristics — especially its comparitive brevity — with the anthems of European countries. Its name is *"la Dessalinienne"* — after Jean Jacques Dessalines (1758–1806), the liberator of this Negro Republic which forms the Western part of the island of Santo Domingo. Dessalines defeated the French under Rocham= beau and on January 1, 1804, he issued a Haitian declaration of independence assuming himself the title of Emperor of Haiti. The anthem was written in 1903 in connection with the country's centennial celebration. The lines are by Justin Lhérisson, the music, by Nicolas Geffrard. Haiti is the only Latin-American republic with French as its official language.

> *Pour le pays, pour les ancêtres,*
> *Marchons unis, marchons unis,*
> *Dans nos rangs point de traîtres,*
> *Du sol soyons seuls maîtres . . .*

(For this land, for our fathers,
One and all, let's march united,
In our ranks we count no traitors,
Of this soil we are the masters . . .)

The *Dessalinienne* was sung for the first time on November 29, 1903, at the *Petit Théatre Sylvain* in Port-au-Prince in com= memoration of the hundredth anniversary of the occupation of Gonaïves.

For fully ten years prior to the creation of the *Dessalinienne*, Haiti had had an unofficial anthem which has survived to this day with the functions of a presidential song. Its origin is curiously in keeping with the spontaneity of its appeal. One day in 1893, a German man-of-war anchored off Port-au-Prince on a good-will

cruise. There were to be festivities on board and the program pre=
pared by the hosts included naturally the national anthem of
Haiti. It would have been fairly embarrassing for the authorities
at Port-au-Prince to admit the truth which was unfortunately that
no Haitian anthem had ever been adopted. Then Occide Jeanty,
a successful musician, proposed to write a tune for Oswald
Durand's patriotic poem, *"Quand nos aïeux brisèrent leurs
entraves"* ("When our fathers broke their fetters"). As the sun
went down over the harbor, while the Haitian flag was lowered
for the night, Jeanty wrote the music which was brilliantly per=
formed the following day on board the German man-of-war.

The anthem of **Honduras** is melodically very similar to that of
Haiti. It begins as follows:

It was selected as the most suitable entry in a public competi=
tion. The text is by Augusto C. Coello (1881–1941). The composer
was Carlos Hartling (1875–1919), an ardent Honduran patriot of
German descent. He organized the first symphony orchestra in
Central America and a number of military bands in the larger
communities of his country. The anthem is characteristically South
American, but the German background of its composer cannot
be concealed. Passages like,

reflect the style of the German *Liedertafel* of the first half of the nineteenth century. The text is an interesting description and inter=pretation of the national flag. It begins

> *Tu bandera, tu bandera*
> *Es un lampo de cielo,*
> *Por un bloque, por un bloque*
> *De nieve cruzado . . .*

> (Lo, the banner of this country
> Has the splendor of the heavens
> While the whiteness of a snowfield
> Cuts across its center . . .)

The text of the **Mexican** anthem is by Francisco González Bocanegra. The composer was Jaime D. Nunó. It was written in 1854 and had its première the same year, on September 16, in Mexico City at the *Teatro de Santa-Anna* which later became known as the National Theater. On this occasion it was sung by the soprano Claudina Fiorenti and the tenor Lorenzo Salvi. The Mexican government had offered a prize for the best poem suitable for an anthem and this was won by the young poet Bocanegra. He was born on January 8, 1824, at San Luis Potosí and died at the youthful age of thirty-seven on April 11, 1861.

On May 17, 1854, Bocanegra's poem had its first public hearing with music by Juan Bottesini. The reaction on the part of the audience was one of complete indifference. Then Mexico City offered a prize of five hundred dollars for the best composition to go with Bocanegra's words. The prize was won by the Spaniard Nunó who at the time was conductor of the National Music Band. He was born in 1824 in Gerona, Catalonia. He left Mexico shortly after the success of his anthem entry and settled down in Buffalo, New York. He died at the advanced age of eighty-four, on July 18, 1908, in Bayside, Queens County, New York. In October, 1942, his mortal remains were taken back to Mexico City where they were laid to rest in great state in the Hall of Heroes which houses also the body of Bocanegra.

No doubt, the Mexican anthem does have a dash and vigor all its own. Its march rhythms are contagious and the modulation to E flat major brings out a particularly solemn quality.

The beginning to be sure, reminds us of an old popular street song which is to be found in the well-known collection, *Die singende Muse an der Pleiße (The Singing Muse on the Pleisse River)* with the text, *"Ihr Schönen höret an"* ("Fair women, listen well"). It was intended to poke fun at the learning of women, and if we may trust the opinion of the musicologist Johann Niko= laus Forkel (1749–1818), one of the best experts on Bach in his time, the composer of it was no one less than Johann Sebastian Bach himself. It is interesting to note that Bach wrote a "Solo per Cembalo" for the album of his wife, Anna Magdalena Bachin, which sounds very much like the song from Sperontes' Pleisse collection. The latter begins as follows:

The German composer Friedrich Wilhelm Kuecken (1810–1882), best known for his song, *"Ach, wie ist's möglich dann"* ("How can I leave thee now"), wrote also the music of *"Wer will unter die Soldaten"* ("He who wants to be a soldier") which is based on the older eighteenth-century tune. It would be utterly absurd to question the authenticity of Nunó's composition, but there must have been some sort of a connection between the two melodies.

The beginning of the Mexican text reads as follows:

Mexicanos, al grito de guerra
El acero aprestad y el bridón,
Y retiemble en sus centros la tierra
Al sonoro rugir del cañón...

(Mexican brethren, at the call of war
Ready your swords, your mount to the fore,
Let the canon rumble and let it roar
Till the echo shake the earth's core...)

The anthem of **Nicaragua** has a tune of uncertain authorship.

Some authorities see in it a variation of a march of the time of Charles III of Spain while others ascribe it to one Anselmo Casti= nove. In any event, the tune was known in the early days of the Nicaraguan Republic and until recently was sung with a text be= ginning

La patria amada canta este día
Su libertad
Y nos recuerda con alegría
Que le debemos amor y paz.

(Beloved fatherland, singing this day
Its liberty,
Reminding all of us joyful and gay
Of our debt of peace and loyalty.)

In 1939, a governmental decree ostracized the old text which was considered poetically inferior and adopted in its stead a poem by Salomón Ibarra Mayorga. Its first stanza reads:

Salve a tí, Nicaragua, en tu suelo
Ya no ruge la voz del cañón,
Ni se tiñe con sangre de hermanos
Tu glorioso pendón bicolor.

(Hail to thee, Nicaragua, on thy soil
No longer roars the voice of canon,
Nor taints, by brothers shed, the brother's blood
The twofold colors of thy glorious flag.)

A song occasionally referred to as a Nicaraguan anthem has the title *"Hermosa soberana"* and begins as follows:

It was written by Blas Villatas and composed by A. Cousin.

The anthem of **Panama** was originally a school song which the composer Santos Jorge A. (1870–1941) arranged for its new func= tions. Jorge was a native of Spain. He went to Panama City in 1889 and stayed there to the time of his death. He composed the *"Himno Istmeño"* which was declared the country's official national anthem in 1903 after the separation of Panama from Colombia. The text of the anthem is by Jerónimo Ossa and begins:

Alcanzamos por fin la victoria
En el campo feliz de la unión,

Con ardientes fulgores de gloria
Se ilumina la nueva nación . . .

(At last we have gathered our triumph
On the happy fields of union
And brilliant flashes of glory
Illumine the newly born nation . . .)

The music is as follows:

It is expressive of patriotic fervor and shares with other South American anthems the division in solo and chorus.

The national anthem of **Paraguay** is variously ascribed to the composers Dupuy and Louis Cavedagni. The text is by Francisco Acuña de Figueroa (1790—1862), a native of Montevideo, poet and chief of the National Library of Uruguay. He also lived for a while in Brazil and Argentina. In addition to the Paraguayan anthem he wrote the text of the anthem of Uruguay. The tune of the former begins as follows:

The first part, the solo, is solemn and dignified. The second part, the chorus, is rather in the nature of Spanish folklore and exhibits a dancelike quality:

The text begins:

> A los pueblos de América infausto
> Tres centurias un cetro oprimió . . .

> (The peoples of hapless America
> For three centuries a scepter oppressed . . .)

The official edition, published by Julio Korn, mentions only the transcription of Remberto Giménez.

The anthem of **Peru** is by José Bernardo Alzedo (1798–1878) whom Slonimsky calls a pioneer of Peruvian music. He wrote a number of sentimental and patriotic songs and also the first Peru= vian theory of music under the title of *Filosofía Elemental de Música*. The words of the anthem are by José Latorre Ugarte (1798 to 1878). It won the prize in a public competition in 1821 but was revised in 1869. At the time the musical revision was handled by Claudio Rebagliati. The suggestive power of the *"Marseillaise"* has influenced the Peruvian anthem like so many other anthems of South America. This is particularly evident in the eighth measure. The text of the Peruvian anthem begins:

> ¡Somos libres! ¡seámoslo siempre!
> Y antes niegue sus luces el Sol,

Que faltemos al voto solemne
Que la Patria al Eterno elevó.

(We are free! Let us be so forever!
May the lights of the sun cease shining
Ere we fail the Almighty
In our country's vow.)

The corresponding music is the choral passage:

The solo, *"Largo tiempo el Peruano oprimido"* ("For a long time the oppressed Peruvian"), begins as follows:

Yet somehow the composer cannot get away from the "Marseil= laise" and he continues

But who would blame him? When the task is to express patriotism in music, it it hard to think of a better model.

The national anthem of **Uruguay** was officially adopted by a governmental decree of July 27, 1848. The music was written by Francisco José Deballi (Debaly), a native of Hungary who came to Uruguay in 1838. He had spent several years in Italy and the influence of Italian opera on his anthem is particularly striking, for the tune is very similar to the chorus of the gondoliers in Donizetti's opera, *Lucrezia Borgia*. But quite apart from this direct link, the anthem of Uruguay is really an operatic aria with a bombastic instrumental introduction whose triplets in thirds with basso figures achieve a resounding effect which is further height= ened by a baldachin of violin tremolos. Solo and chorus share the dramatic melody which has everything — from coloratura passages to chromatic alterations — that a lover of opera might ask for.

The text by Francisco Acuña de Figueroa, who also wrote the anthem of Paraguay, begins

> *¡Orientales, la patria o la tumba!*
> *¡Libertad, o con gloria morir!*

> (Orientals! The grave or our country!
> We want freedom or glorious death!)

The term "Oriental" has of course nothing to do with the Orient. The official name of Uruguay is *República Oriental del Uruguay*, that is, Oriental or Eastern Republic of the Uruguay River, and hence the word Oriental signifies also Uruguayan.

The music of the vocal portion begins:

The national anthem of **Venezuela** is the oldest of all Latin-American anthems. Its text is by Vicente Salias, the music by Juan José Landaeta. It was conceived in the wake of the country's early attempts to gain its independence. These were crushed and in due course both the composer and the poet were executed (1814). Their work was given the official status of a national anthem by a government decree of May 25, 1881. Now and again one finds that the Venezuelan anthem is ascribed to the pianist Teresa Carreño, the "Valkyrie of the Piano," as she has been called. However, she composed only a hymn for the Bolívar Centennary and not the Venezuelan *Marseillaise*. The text of the latter begins with the chorus:

> *Gloria al bravo pueblo*
> *Que el yugo lanzó,*
> *La ley respetando,*
> *La virtud y honor.*

> (Be glory to the people
> That bravely broke its yoke,
> With due respèct to law,
> To virtue and to honor.)

The music begins:

This anthem is musically different from the other Latin-American anthems. Going back to the beginning of the nineteenth century, the "Venezuelan *Marseillaise*" did not arise under the stars of the Italian opera. Much rather might it be said to show kinship with German folk music. It is not possible to overlook in it a certain lack of organic coherence. But this detail would not seem to have interfered with the strong impact which its patriotic force has been exerting for almost a century and a half.

A round-table conference, which closed at the Hague on June 3, 1954, accorded **Surinam** (Dutch Guiana) as well as the Netherlands Antilles the status of semi-autonomous overseas dominions as a reform of their earlier status of Dutch colonies. The Netherlanders of Surinam sing as their anthem the *"Surinaamse Volkslied"* ("Song of the People of Surinam"). Its text had been written in 1893 by C. A. Hoikstra to go with a tune composed in 1876 by C. de Puy. Neither de Puy nor Hoikstra ever considered the possibility that their song might win official recognition. The opening measures of the tune are strongly reminiscent of the German children's song, *"Wer will unter die Soldaten"* ("If you want to be a soldier").

The parliamentary state of **Trinidad** and **Tobago** was established in 1962. It consists of two islands in the Lesser Antilles with a population of Negroes, Whites, East Indians, and Chinese. Trinidad was discovered in 1498 by Columbus. It subsequently became a Spanish settlement. In 1797 it was conquered by the British. Trinidad belonged to the West Indian Federation. The present national anthem of Trinidad and Tobago was originally intended for that federation. It is the work of Patrick S. Castagne.

The text of the anthem begins:

> Forged from the love of liberty,
> In the fires of hope and prayer
> With boundless faith in our destiny . . .

This brings to a close our survey of the national anthems of South America. The homogeneity of South American culture is manifest also in the domain of the national anthem which on the whole reveals the influence of the heroic style of the contemporary Italian opera, that being the style of music best equipped to excite the hearts and heads of the actors on the historical stage of the movement for independence of the South American republics.

UNITED STATES OF AMERICA

Of the various national songs of the **United States,** only the "Star-Spangled Banner" is officially recognized as a national anthem, but several of the others are hardly less popular.

The "Star-Spangled Banner" goes back to the year 1814, that is, to the time of the war against Britain in the course of which the Americans found themselves in dire straits when on August 25 British troops occupied Washington and burned down the Capitol, the White House, and almost all the other public buildings as well.

The well-known story of the origin of the song is briefly sum= marized as follows. Near Baltimore the British had arrested a certain civilian whom they kept on board a man-of-war. A friend of his, Francis Scott Key, came up with a white flag to arrange for the prisoner's release. The matter was settled to everyone's satis= faction, but while Key was on board, the boat had to carry out a night bombardment of Fort McHenry. It was the sight of Old Glory above the fort heroically withstanding the bombardment that inspired Key to write his immortal lines.

The first public mention of the song is found in the *Baltimore American* of September 21, 1814, but an exact and authentic report on its genesis was contributed by the poet himself in talking to his brother-in-law, Mr. R. B. Taney, subsequently Chief Justice of the U. S. Supreme Court. In 1856, when Henry V. D. Jones pre= pared his edition of the *Poems of the Late Francis S. Key, Esq.* (New York, 1857), he was in a position to base his account on Taney's immediate authority.

The questions as to who sang the song first and how its tune came to be adapted to it, are hopelessly bogged down in moot polemics. It is, however, an established fact that the very first report on the song does identify the tune to be used with it. It was the tune of "To Anacreon in Heaven," a song imported from England and at the time generally known in America.

"To Anacreon in Heaven" was the official song of the Anac= reontic Society of London, a sort of social-musical-masonic club which had been founded in or shortly after 1771 and whose existence petered out between the years 1791 and 1794. When Haydn was in London (1791), he was the guest of honor of the Anacreontics whose group had the reputation of being very ex= clusive but excellent company. The Anacreontic Society met at the Crown and Anchor Tavern on the Strand. Ralph Tomlinson, one of the presidents of the organization, was also the author of the song, "To Anacreon in Heaven," the first stanza of which begins as follows:

> To Anacreon in Heaven, where he sat in full glee,
> A few sons of harmony sent a petition,
> That he their inspirer and patron would be; ...

The song has six stanzas. Everyone ends with a variant of the couplet,

> And, besides, I'll instruct ye, like me, to intwine
> The myrtle of Venus with Bacchus's vine.

The composer who contributed a tune to this song with the simple title, "Anacreontic Society," was John Stafford Smith (1750—1836), a British musician, conductor, and organist. He was very well known in his time, principally through his "catches" for some of which he received prizes from the London Catch Club. Some of his songs too, as for instance "Since Phillis has bubbled" and "Blest pair of syrens," were very successful and contributed greatly to his popularity. Actually Smith's name has a well-earned place in the annals of musicology, for he was one of Sir John Hawkins' collaborators on his famous *General History of the Science and Practice of Music* (1776), and the author of *Musica Antiqua*.

John Stafford would certainly never have dreamed that one of his songs, the one "To Anacreon in Heaven," would eventually be sung by millions and millions of American patriots as their national anthem. But even before that came to pass, the popular success of the tune had been quite extraordinary. It was sung in all parts of the British Isles and soon also in America. We may assume that it was used as the "fraternity song" of the Columbian Anacreontic Society which was founded in New York City in 1795. According to one comtemporary source it was sung by a certain Mr. West in a concert he gave in Savannah, Georgia, on August 19, 1796. It will also be found in a large number of early American "songsters," as songbooks of popular appeal were called at the time.

One special reason for the popularity of the song in America may be the fact that from a very early time it was used as a masonic song. In this respect we may recall that the British National Anthem was also used in masonic lodges.

It appeared in a book entitled *A Selection of Masonic Songs . . . Arranged with Choruses in Parts, and Respectfully Dedicated to the Brethren of the Most Ancient & Honourable Fraternity of Free and Accepted Masons, By Br. S. Holden.* According to Sonneck, who bases his information on sources drawn from Grattan Flood and Frank Kidson, Smollet Holden published this book in 1795 or 1796. However, in the copy owned by the Indiana University Library I could find no date of publication, and an earlier date than that proposed by Sonneck should not be excluded.

The masonic text, which corresponds to the text of "To Anacreon in Heaven," may be interesting:

No. XXVII.

Song and Chorus, Written by Br. Connel, on behalf of the Masonic Orphan School.

To old Hiram in Heav'n where he sat in full Glee
A few brother Masons sent up a petition,
That He their inspirer and Patron would be,

To help Masons Orphans, and mend their condition,
The Gods were all mute, when he mention'd our suit,
They gave their consent, and donations to boot.
(Chorus)
Then who would not wish, like Celestials divine,
In a cause, like the present, to cheerfully join.

There is no doubt that Francis Scott Key knew the words and the music of the Anacreon song. Its meter and rhythm must have been in the back of his mind when he jotted down his patriotic lines. At any rate, the very first printing of the poem bore the notation, "Tune: To Anacreon in Heaven."

There is a tradition which asserts that Joseph Hopper Nicholson — a judge whose critical opinion Key consulted the day after he had written the song — was responsible for the selection of the tune. But it seems more likely that Key had made his choice long before he went to see Nicholson.

As holds true for almost all the major national anthems, in the case of the "Star-Spangled Banner" too there were doubts and disputes in regard to where the credit for the melody should go. It was, for instance, ascribed to the British composer Dr. Samuel Arnold (1740—1802) who for a time was the music master of the Anacreontic Society. Then again it was claimed as an Irish folk song, but today there is fairly general agreement that Smith was the composer and that the original version ran as follows:

This tune — taken from the London collection, *The Vocal Enchantress* of 1783 — has as its most striking characteristic a very wide vocal range. One feels tempted to suggest that it was originally conceived for instrumental performance. In a version of 1785 it is arranged as a glee, that is, an unaccompanied song for three solo voices. The melody proper is sung by a basso; two tenor voices respond.

In course of time the "Star-Spangled Banner" underwent various changes. The third stanza was left out because of its anti-British sentiment. As a matter of fact, a certain Dr. Spowers tried to replace it by an eminently pro-British stanza.

The tune was transformed too. A hundred and fifty years ago it did not sound as it does today. It was originally written in the same heroic style as "Rule Britannia" with which it has certain affinities in the concluding phrases. It is indeed remarkable that this Old-English style of heroic music should have survived in the "Star-Spangled Banner," just as though we were to be assured in this symbolic way that the ancient ideals of Great Britain are embodied in the new ideas of the United States.

The anthem, sung a million times by millions of people, has naturally been drawn into the orbit of higher music where it is found in numerous quotations. I remember an amusing incident which occurred on a Dutch steamer in 1939 when I traveled from

Rotterdam to New York. The band was playing the "Star-Spangled Banner" when a lady exclaimed, "Oh, I know that. It's from 'Madame Butterfly'." She evidently knew the song only from Puccini's opera where it functions as a sort of leitmotiv which characterizes the hero of the fable who is an American officer.

Some time ago Toscanini produced a new version of Verdi's "Hymn of the Nations," and he put at the end of it the "International" together with the "Star-Spangled Banner."

This American song is doubtless one of the great national anthems. It was officially adopted as the National Anthem of the United States by an act of Congress in 1931.

Among the other national songs of the United States, the most popular is "Yankee Doodle" which is also well known abroad. The first printed record of the tune as a whole is that in James Aird's collection, *Selection of Scotch, English, Irish, and Foreign Airs for the Fife, Violin, or German Flute,* which appeared in 1782 in Glasgow. It runs there as follows:

It appeared in slightly changed versions in various ballad operas of the time. It was sung for instance by the then famous John Edwin in his part of Dickey Ditto in the opera *Two to One* (1784) by Samuel Arnold (1740—1802). The text began, "Adzooks, old

Crusty, why so rusty?" Another version appeared in 1788 in Charles Dibdin's *Musical Tour* with the text, "I sing Ulysses and those chiefs."

It is to be noted that the tune appeared in Aird's above-mentioned collection in a group of American songs like "Negro Jig" and "Virginia Melody." This would permit the conjecture that it actually originated some time earlier in the American colonies, was brought to England, and then returned again to the New World.

The earliest printed record of it in the United States is apparently the *Federal Overture* which the New York musician and publisher Benjamin Carr (1768—1831) arranged and brought out in 1794. So far no copy of this edition has been located. All we have of it is a potpourri for two flutes in the fifth series of Shaw & Carr's *Gentle= man's Amusement*. This march (or overture) includes items like the "Carmagnole" and the "Marseillaise" and thus — being a sort of compilation of national anthems — might be called a minor precursor of Verdi's *Hymn of the Nations*. The first separate edition of the song with an adapted text appeared in 1798 in Philadelphia over the imprint of G. Willig. It was combined with the "President's March" or "Hail Columbia" and had a text be= ginning, "Columbians all, the present hour . . ."

There have been attempts to trace the history of the tune back to the French wars in the middle of the eighteenth century. Yet they all have come to nought, and it does not seem possible to trace the exact origin of the song. One thing is certain: the British used it to make fun of the Yankees, and the Yankees in turn — a case by no means unique in the history of national music — adopted it as an expression of their own patriotic fervor. When the New England= ers congregated at night in their churches to sing their psalms and hymns, British soldiers outside would often attempt to disturb and insult them by singing the "Yankee Doodle." When Lord Percy's troops left Boston in 1775 to catch John Hancock and Samuel Adams, they sang it with the lines:

Yankee Doodle came to town
For to buy a firelock:
We will tar and feather him
And so we will John Hancock.

But it also worked the other way round. As early as 1770 it was
sung to jeer the British with the words:

Yankee Doodle came to town
Riding on a pony,
Stuck a feather in his cap
And called it macaroni.

In which connection it need hardly be pointed out that macaroni
is nothing to eat but most probably "a member of a class of trav=
eled young British dandies."

A text replete with regionalisms and slang appeared in Boston
and remained in vogue for many years. It began:

Father and I went down to camp
Along with Captain Gooding;
There we see the men and boys
As thick as hasty-pudding.
(Chorus)
Yankee doodle keep it up
Yankee doodle dandy,
Mind the music and the step,
And with the girls be handy.

The most popular form of the tune is the following which also
appears in Sousa's National Airs (1900):

Like many another national song, the "Yankee Doodle" has re=
peatedly been used as a theme for variations. So for instance by
Anton Rubinstein, Henri Vieuxtemps (*Caprice burlesque*, op. 17),
and Daniel G. Mason (*In the Styles of Various Composers*). Some
critics are inclined to discern the "Yankee Doodle" also in the last
movement of Dvořák's *New World Symphony*.

The third national song of the United States is "Hail Columbia."
Its origin is linked up with the Franco-American tension of 1798
which almost precipitated a shooting war. The text was written by
Joseph Hopkinson, a young lawyer whose father, Francis Hopkin=
son, was the first native American composer mentioned in the
records of history. The author himself has left us the following
account of how he came to write the song. His expression, "our
city," refers to Philadelphia; the "young man" is Gilbert Fox.

"Hail Columbia" was written in the summer of 1798, when
war with France was thought to be inevitable. Congress was
then in session in Philadelphia, debating upon that important
subject, and acts of hostility had actually taken place. The
contest between England and France was still raging, and the
people of the United States were divided into parties for the
one side or the other, some thinking that policy and duty
required us to espouse the cause of "republican France" as she
was called, while others were for connecting ourselves with
England, under the belief that she was the great preservative
power of good principles and safe government. The violation
of our rights by both belligerents was forcing us from the just
and wise policy of President Washington, which was to do
equal justice to both but to part with neither, and to preserve
an honest and strict neutrality between them. The prospect of
a rupture with France was exceedingly offensive to the portion
of the people who espoused her cause, and the violence of the

spirit of party had never risen higher, I think not so high, in our country, as it did at that time upon that question.

The theatre was then open in our city. A young man be= longing to it, whose talent was high as a singer, was about to take a benefit. I had known him when he was at school. On this acquaintance he called on me one Saturday afternoon, his benefit being announced for the following Monday. His pro= spects were very disheartening; but he said that if he could get a patriotic song adapted to the "President's March" he did not doubt a full house; that the poets of the theatrical corps had been trying to accomplish it, but had not succeeded. I told him I would try what I could do for him. He came the next afternoon, and the song, such as it is, was ready for him The object of the author was to get up an American spirit which should be independent of, and above the interests, pas= sion and policy of both belligerents, and look and feel ex= clusively for our honor and rights. No allusion is made to France or England, or the quarrel between them, or to the question of which was most in fault in their treatment of us. Of course the song found favor with both parties, for both were American, at least neither could disown the sentiments and feelings it indicated. Such is the history of this song, which has endured infinitely beyond the expectation of the author, as it is beyond any merit it can boast of except that of being truly and exclusively patriotic in its sentiment and spirit.

The melody of "Hail Columbia" — known as the "President's March" — was presumably written during the presidency of George Washington and designed to replace the "Washington March" of the days of the Revolution. According to an account by William McKoy of 1829, the March was written by Johannes Roth, a Ger= man who died in 1804. Some modern authorities call him Philip Roth. Another view ascribes the authorship of the March to Philip Phile, also a German, who lived in Philadelphia from 1784 on and died there in 1793. Modern musicologists are inclined to support Phile's claims: The text, as it appeared in 1798 in Willig's *Musical Magazine*, reads as follows:

> Hail! Columbia happy land
> hail! ye Heros heav'n born band,
> who fought and bled in freedom's cause
> who fought and bled in freedom's cause
> and when the storm of war was gone

enjoy'd the peace your valor won;
let Independence be our boast,
ever mindful what it cost,
ever grateful for the prize
let its Altar reach the Skies.
Firm, united, let us be
rallying round our Liberty,
as a band of Brothers join'd
peace and safety we shall find.

The historian of American music, John T. Howard, insists that
no matter what may be said about the "Star-Spangled Banner,"
"Yankee Doodle," and "Hail Columbia," the song which is "truly
our national hymn" is the song which all the world knows by the
name of "America."

My country 'tis of Thee,
Sweet land of liberty,
Of thee I sing.
Land where my fathers died,
Land of the Pilgrim's pride,
From ev'ry mountain side
Let freedom ring.

Still, as every musically-minded person will immediately rec=
ognize, these lines were written to the tune of the British Royal
Anthem, "God Save the King." The author of "America" was
Samuel Francis Smith (1808–1895), a minister of the Gospel. The
year of its composition was 1832. It is interesting to note that
Smith found the tune not in a British but in a German songbook.
According to his own account, a friend of his had brought back
with him from a trip abroad a number of German songbooks, and
in one of them he found the tune — presumably with the title "Heil
Dir im Siegerkranz" — which he immediately singled out for his
poem. This happened in Andover, Mass. The song was first
published in Mason's The Choir of 1832. The song's popularity
kept growing over the years. It has no rival but the "Star-Spangled
Banner" itself.

COMMONWEALTH OF NATIONS

The British anthem was the anthem not only of Britain but of the British Empire. The countries forming the Empire had in many cases their own individual anthems as well. The relative popularity of these in comparison with that of "God save the King" could well be taken as an index of the lesser or fuller integration of the various countries with the Empire.

The Commonwealth of Nations is no Empire. Most of its twenty-two affiliates are psychologically and politically as little subordinate to it as the member states of other international organizations feel subordinate to them.

In this book the members of the Commonwealth appear scattered throughout its chapters as they appear geographically scattered over the globe. Preserved in this closing chapter are those countries whose links to Britain are popularly felt to be — with considerable historical justification — especially close and intimate.

If **Australia** has no official national anthem of its own, it does have the famous "Waltzing Matilda" which does for the Austra=lians at least as much as more solemn official anthems can possibly do for the citizens of other countries.

It has been adopted as a regimental march by the Queen's Royal Second Foot Regiment of the British Army stationed in Berlin. During World War II it was sung wherever Australian military forces gathered and was extremely popular with Americans. The song begins with the immortal line, "Once a jolly swagman camped by a billabong." As a true ballad it goes on to relate how this swagman, always in search of work and shelter, boils his "billy" (a receptacle for holding water) by the "billabong" (a water hole).

Then a "jumbuck" (sheep) comes to the water hole to drink. The swagman kills it and stores the meat in his "tucker-bag" (food bag). He is caught in the act by the "squatter" (ranch owner) and the troopers charge him. Rather than be taken alive, the swagman leaps into the "billabong" and is drowned. The lyrics end by pointing out that "his ghost may be heard as you pass by that billabong."

The author of this ballad is Andrew Barton ("Banjo") Paterson, who died in 1941 at the age of 76. The text, in its original form, reflects the resentment of the early settlers against the squatters who held large tracts of land. It was written specifically for the tune which is an old Scottish melody and inspired Paterson — as the story goes — when he heard Mary Macpherson play it on the auto-harp. The setting which is current today is the work of Marie Cowan.

Close to the hearts of all patriotic Australians is also the song "Advance Australia Fair" with music by P. D. McCormick. Its style reflects typically mid-nineteenth-century popular music. The triadic structure of the melody gives it a touch of solemnity and dignity.

A national song of **New Zealand** which might well be con= sidered a national anthem is "God Defend New Zealand." It is sung on all special occasions. The text was written by Thomas Bracken (1843–1898). The first stanza reads as follows:

> God of Nations! at Thy feet
> In the bonds of love we meet;

Hear our voices we entreat,
God defend our Free land,
Guard Pacific's triple star
From the shafts of strife and war,
Make her praises heard afar,
God defend New Zealand.

Thomas Bracken was born in Ireland, but went to New Zealand early in life. There he engaged primarily in newspaper work, although for a time he was member of Parliament. He wrote "God defend New Zealand" in 1878. The *Saturday Advertiser* offered a prize for the best musical setting of it. The winning entry was by John J. Woods (1849—1934), an Australian, who was teaching at the time in New Zealand. It is a very simple marching song with a choral refrain.

The original edition was published by Charles Begg and Co., Ltd,. of Wellington, New Zealand, with both English and Maori texts.

The text of the **Canadian** anthem was written in French by Adolphe B. Routhier (1839—1920). The music is by Calixa Lavallée (1842—1891), a native of Verchères in the province of Quebec. He died in Boston where he had settled down as a concert pianist and music teacher after a successful traveling career. During the Civil War he was in the United States and fought on the side of the North. In 1874 he became the director of the Grand Opera House in New York, the predecessor of the Metropolitan Opera House. He wrote "O Canada" in 1880 at the request of prominent French-Canadian patriotic societies.

"O Canada" represents rather the introvert and prayerlike type of anthem. The melody seems expressive of the country's peaceful character and the religious attitude of its people.

> *O Canada! Terre de nos aïeux,*
> *Ton front est ceint de fleurons glorieux!*
> *Car ton bras sait porter l'épée,*
> *Il sait porter la croix!*
> *Ton histoire est une épopée*
> *Des plus brillants exploits.*
> *Et ta valeur, de foi trempée,*
> *Protégera nos foyers et nos droits,*
> *Protégera nos foyers et nos droits.*

> (O Canada! Thou land our fathers found,
> Thy crown we see of glorious flowers wound.
> Thy arm to hold the sword is strong,
> Is strong the cross to hold.
> Thy history is one great song
> Of brilliant feats untold.
> Our homes, our rights to us belong.
> Shielded by valor which thy faith made bold,
> Shielded by valor which thy faith made bold.)

There is also an English text by Robert Stanley Weir (1856 to 1926). It begins, "O Canada! Our home and native land." It is not a translation of Routhier's lines but was written — as the author put it himself (1908) — "because Mr. Lavallée's splendid melody (one worthy to rank with the finest national airs of any of the older lands) has hitherto lacked an English setting in the song style."

If the national airs of these former Dominions emphasize the autonomy of the members of the British Commonwealth of Nations, "God Save the King" continues to bind them together. We began this discussion of the world's national anthems with Carey's old tune and now have returned to it at the end of our discussion. It is the tune most often heard not only in America but throughout the world. From among all national anthems the one with the least pronounced national character, the one with the least melodic and rhythmic "pep" is the most international, the most popular, the most far-spread. This observation — if we are so inclined — may fill us with a certain political optimism. The commonly human — in music at least—seems to prevail over the idiosyncratically national. If one and the same melody is sung time and again by millions of men, then its power must in the end produce tangible effects of harmony, unification, homogeneity, and mutual balance.

We need a world anthem, a melody which can inspire us in brotherly respect to keep our faith in friendship and in love. After the horrible years of war, of hatred and destruction, an anthem of peace must be found for all peoples of all lands.

Where is the poet, where is the composer whose genius can pro= duce the anthem of humanity for all the millions for whom Beethoven sang after the years of hate of the Napoleonic wars,

> *Seid umschlungen Millionen,*
> *Diesen Kuß der ganzen Welt . . .*

> (Be embraced you throng of millions,
> and this kiss to all the World)?

APPENDIX OF NOTES

[1] In view of the importance of this song, some further historical details may be welcome at this point. The author is indebted for them to Oswald Redlich and Viktor Junk who published an article in German on "The Song of Prince Eugene" in the *Bulletin of the Academy of the Sciences in Vienna* (Philosophical-Historical Class). The origin of the song — as that of many of its peers — is a subject on which legend appears to have more to say than history. There is, for instance, the story launched by one D. Stratil and based purportedly on old documents discovered in Moravia, that a certain Michel Mages enlisted in 1683 in an Austrian regiment which took part in the wars against the Turks. During the siege of Belgrade in 1688, Michel Mages — according to this story — composed the song of Prince Eugene which subsequently came to be sung more and more by the soldiers in the field, especially again at Belgrade in 1717 at which time the last two stanzas were added. By way of a proper climax, Stratil's story has Prince Eugene take delight in the song and convey the expression of his gratitude and applause to its writer. It would seem that this story was made out of whole cloth. In any event, the text of *"Prinz Eugenius"* is clearly affiliated to earlier songs. There is, for instance, a song dealing with the freeing of Vienna from the Turks in 1683 which has the opening lines:

> *Als Kursachsen dies vernommen,*
> *Daß der Türk' vor Wien was kommen,*
> *Ruft er seine Völker bald.*
> *Tät sich eilends dahin machen,*
> *Da hört man das Pulver krachen,*
> *Da wurden viel Bluthunde kalt.*

(And the Saxon Prince Elector,
Told that Turks were in that sector;
To Vienna sent his men.
And he joined them in the battle,
Were one heard the powder crackle,
And cooled the bloodhounds there and then.)

The leading idea of the song of *"Prinz Eugen"* was adopted
and emulated in many later war songs, as for instance in one with
Laudon at Belgrade in 1789 as its hero, in the songs of "Archduke
Charles" of 1796 and 1799, and in a Radetzky song of 1849. The
echo of it can even be heard in a war song of 1870 with the lines:

Als Napoleon dies vernommen,
Ließ er gleich die Stiefel kommen.

(When Napoleon heard this story,
"Get my boots," he cried, "and hurry!")

In addition to this famous song there are quite a few other
texts dealing with the Prince of Savoy, such as the one on the
Battle of Senta, the occupation of Lille, the battle of Petrovaradin,
and the fall of Timisoara in 1716.

Quite often the conquest of a fortress is compared to the
"conquest" of a lady. So, for instance, the "fair lady Lille" puts
up a determined resistance against the attacker but is forced before long to surrender.

All these songs are concerned with the Austrian armies in
which the most diverse European peoples were represented, including the Hungarians, Bohemians, Poles, and many others.
Yet, it is a uniform trait of them that they regard the Empire as
German in its essence. The armies are armies of the *German*
emporer, and it is *German* bravery which is being glorified. Thus
we are confronted with the paradox that the French Prince
Eugene appears as a German hero, the "Mars" of the Germans.
It is remarkable, indeed, that all these songs reflect an emotional

engagement in a *German* empire. This would seem to be reason enough to regard the song of Prince Eugene as one of the earliest national anthems, even though the nationalism expressed in it—in contrast to that of the later anthems—is quite spontaneous, undogmatic, and possibly "unconscious." The rhythm of this song is that of a so-called "double," i. e., a folk dance in alternating measure of the kind frequently encountered in Bavaria and Bohemia. In his study, "The old Bavarian Marsker Dance as the prototype of the melody of the Song of Prince Eugene," the historian Viktor Junk traces the tune to the old Bavarian Marsker or Marushka dance which appears to have survived far into the nineteenth century. The connection of the tune of the Song of Prince Eugene with the old moriscoes or Moorish dances with their aggressive rhythm confirms additionally the internationalism of the song. (Cf. Paul Nettl, *"Die Moresca,"* Archiv für Musik-Wissenschaft, XIV.)

[2] Elsewhere too the French have allowed foreign elements to infiltrate their music. One of the most significant musicians after Lully, the aforementioned Campra (1660–1744), who for decades dominated the French opera, was the son of a surgeon who had moved to France from Turin. It is a sort of comedy of errors that the Italian Casanova confessed to be bored to death by an opera which had the character of a *divertissement* and was hence French but which the composer, a half-Italian and hence half-countryman of Casanova, had based on Italian (Venetian) motifs. Such things can hardly be explained without recourse to factors of patriotism and nationalism. In later times, too, "foreigners" appear repeatedly in the history of French music. Finally, César Franck (1822–1890), although born in Liège, was at least in part of German descent.

[3] I have been told by Professor K. B. Jirák, who is one of the foremost Czech composers and who witnessed these events from a vantage point lending weight to his judgment, that the scandal

was clearly of fascist origin. At the time the Czech followers of German National Socialism were beginning to throw their weight around.

⁴ All these things are most intimately related to the importance one may feel inclined to ascribe in political terms to the so-called exchange activities in the cultural domain. The great foundations have been encouraged by various government agencies to contribute substantial sums for the promotion of "good-neighborly" music. At times one cannot but wonder whether these South-American states—in purely musical terms—do in fact deserve such support. During the Hitler era, when the Czechs wished to "appease" the Sudeten Germans, the attempt was made to build up a sort of "Sudeten-German music," and the German transmitter which was financed by the Czech government (the Eduard-Beneš transmitter) tried to present as much as possible works by Sudeten-German composers. These compositions were less than ephemeral. Today they are completely forgotten.

⁵ It may be objected at this point that the Czechs are Central Europeans and that Prague has always been regarded as the heart of Europe. But the proximity of the Germans has at all times put the Czechs on their guard and strengthened their national consciousness possibly beyond the norm among other peoples of Europe. More characteristic rhythms than those of Dvořák and Smetana can hardly be found elsewhere in Europe, and that is the reason which obliges us to speak of the Czechs in musical terms as a "peripheral people."

⁶ In my book, *Dance and Dance Music* (in German; Freiburg, 1962), I have pointed out that the word *"chaconne"* does not come from *cada uno* or from *ciascuno* but may be traced to the name of an old Peruvian dance which was known as the *"guacona."*

⁷ The fame of the anthem did not protect it from but may in fact

have laid it open to being parodied. Unpopular originals rarely engender parodies. Edward VII did not like the anthem. He thought it sounded like a dirge. George V is reported to have claimed that it reminded him of a "jig." Of the many parodies, the following goes back to the time of the French Revolution:

> Long live great Guillotine
> Who shaves the head so clean
>   of Queen and King;
> Whose power is so great
> That ev'ry tool of State
> Dreadeth his mighty weight,
> Wonderful Thing!

From time to time there are voices to be heard in Britain calling for a new anthem. The point is made that the anthem gets played too often and hence is heard too much. "If the anthem is to regain more of its meaning, it must be heard less frequently," wrote the *Evening Standard*. Then there is, of course, the matter of the succession in which the sex of the monarch may shift. In 1953, when Queen Elizabeth II came to the throne, the text of the first stanza was changed as follows:

> God save our gracious Queen,
> Long live our noble Queen,
> God save the Queen.
> Send her victorious,
> Happy and glorious,
> Long to reign over us.
> God save the Queen.

This version, in fact, had already been in use under Queen Victoria. The result is a sort of "inferiority complex" affecting the anthem, for people seem to prefer to pay homage to the "father" rather than the "mother of their country." This may explain the parodies recited in Britain in a whisper or aloud. One

such was in fact broadcast as part of the BBC television show
"Twenty-four Hours":

> Oh, close our trading gap
> And make the chap
> Buy British now.
> Keep Sterling proud and free
> At Dollar parity
> So without too much effort, we
> May live somehow.
>
> Oh, keep the gnomes at bay
> Let Lombard Street hold sway
> As nature planned.
> Let exports quickly soar,
> Let imports hit the floor
> So that Britannia rules once more
> With cash in hand.

Such versions cannot but affect adversely the venerable standing of the anthem, and it is hardly surprising that the tune is
being heard less and less often. While in the past the anthem
was heard at Covent Garden and in all the great theaters at the
beginning and at the end of every performance, it now is heard
only on special occasions and to mark the opening of the season.

[8] We have pointed out that the British Royal anthem is the
oldest national anthem. In the present context, however, we must
not fail to mention that the French anthem had a precursor as
early as the sixteenth century. In 1589, when Henry III died, his
successor was Henry IV, victor in the battle of Coutras (1587)
during the War of the Huguenots. These events inspired the
text, "*Vive Henri IV, Vive ce roi vaillant*" ["Long live this valiant
king, Henry IV"]. The tune was, interestingly, derived from a
dance. It is that of a "*branle coupé*" with the title "Cassandra"
to be found in the treatise on dancing, "*Orchésographie*," by

Thoinot Arbeau (1588). (For a musical quotation, see Böhme, *op. cit.*, p. 42.)

⁹ Today the Maritza song is by no means forgotten, but it was replaced by a new national anthem through an edict of the Presidium of the People's Assembly of December 30, 1950. The new anthem is a cooperative product. The text was composed by Nikola Furnadshiew, Miaden Issaew, and Elissaweta Bagrjana, while the music was composed by Georgi Dimitrow, Georgi Zlatew-Tscherkin, and Swetoslaw Obretenow. The song was chosen on the basis of a contest organized by the government. The tune, which consists of two parts, is marchlike, but there is nothing particularly characteristic about it.

It is not hard to understand that the Maritza song has not been displaced.

¹⁰ The "International" continues to be regarded as the song of the Communist Party of the Soviet Union.

BIBLIOGRAPHY

Note: The following list of titles is intended to be suggestive rather than comprehensive. It serves simultaneously to identify the more important items of marginal interest to which brief reference is made in the text proper.

Adler, Guido (ed.), *Handbuch der Musikgeschichte* . . ., 2 vols., Berlin-Wilmersdorf, 1930 (2nd edition). See also page 131 above.

Aird, James (ed.), *Selection of Scotch, English, Irish, and Foreign Airs* . . ., Glasgow, 1782. See also page 175 above.

Amhurst, Nicholas (ed.), *pseudonym* Caleb d'Anvers, *The Crafts= man*, London, 1731—1737. See also page 17 above.

Anvers, Caleb d', *see* Amhurst, Nicholas.

Böhme, Franz Magnus (ed.), *Volksthümliche Lieder der Deutschen im 18. und 19. Jahrhundert* . . ., Leipzig, 1895. See also page 76 above.

Bohn, Emil, *Die Nationalhymnen der europäischen Völker*, Bres= lau, 1908. See also pages 83, 114 above.

Botstiber, Hugo, *see* Pohl, Carl Ferdinand.

Burney, Charles, *The Present State of Music in Germany, the Netherlands, and United Provinces* . . ., London, 1773 (1st edition), 1775 (2nd edition). See also pages 13, 38, 42 above.

Chappell, William, *Popular Music of the Olden Time* . . ., 2 vols., London, 1859.

Clark, Richard, *An Accound of the National Anthem Entitled God Save the King!* . . ., London, 1822.

Clark, Richard (ed.), *Words of the Most Favourite Pieces Performed at the Glee Club, the Catch Club, & Other Public Societies*, London, 1814.

Cummings, William Hayman, *God Save the King: the Origin and History of the Music and Words of the National Anthem*, London and New York, 1902. See also page 37 above.

Dibdin, Charles, *The Musical Tour of Mr. Dibdin . . .*, Sheffield, 1788. See also page 176 above.

Dibdin, Edward Rimbault, "The Bi-Centennary of Rule Britannia," *Music and Letters*, 1940. See also page 48 above.

Fiaux, Louis, *la Marseillaise, son histoire dans l'histoire des français depuis 1792 . . .*, Paris, 1918.

Finley, Lorraine Noel, *see* Treharne, Bryceson.

Franck, Melchior (ed.), *Opusculum etlicher newer und alter Reuter-Liedlein*, 1603. See also page 91 above.

Fuller Maitland, John Alexander, *The Musical Association Lec= tures*, 1917.

Gradenwitz, Peter, *The Music of Israel; its Rise and Growth Through 5000 Years*, New York, 1949. See also page 137 above.

Grétry, André Modeste, *Mémoires, ou essais sur la musique*, Paris, 1797. See also pages 74, 75 above.

Grout, Donald Jay, *A Short History of Opera*, New York, 1947.

Hadow, William Henry, *A Croatian Composer; Notes Toward the Study of Joseph Haydn*, London, 1897. See also pages 56, 59 above.

Heuss, Alfred, "Haydn's Kaiserhymne," *Zeitschrift für Musikwis= senschaft*, I. See also page 59 above.

Idelsohn, Abraham Zebi (ed.), *Thesaurus of Oriental Hebrew Melodies*, 10 vols., Leipzig, 1914—1933. See also page 23 above.

Istel, Edgar, "Die Marseillaise, eine deutsche Melodie?," *Die Musik*, XVII, 1925. See also pages 73, 75 above.

Key, Francis Scott, *Poems of the Late Francis S. Key, Esq.; with an Introductory Letter by Chief Justice Taney*, New York, 1857. See also page 170 above.

Kitchener, William (ed.), *The Loyal and National Songs of Eng= land*, London, 1823.

Koeckert, *Rouget de Lisle und seine Stellung in der Geschichte der Musik*, 1898.

Kretzschmar, Hermann, *Geschichte des neuen deutschen Liedes*, Leipzig, 1911. See also page 6 above.

Kretzschmar, Hermann, *Geschichte der Oper*, Leipzig, 1919.

Kuháč, Franjo Šaver, *Josip Haydn i Hrvatské Národne Popievke*, Agram, 1880. See also pages 56, 57, 58 above.

Leitzmann, Albert (ed.), *Wolfgang Amadeus Mozart; Berichte der Zeitgenossen und Briefe* . . ., Leipzig, 1926.

Le Roy de Sainte Croix, François Noël, *le Chant de guerre pour l'armée du Rhin ou la Marseillaise* . . ., Strasbourg, 1880.

Le Roy de Sainte Croix, François Noël, *la Marseillaise et Rouget de Lisle* . . ., Strasbourg, 1880.

Loth, Arthur, *le Chant de la Marseillaise, son véritable auteur* . . ., Paris, 1886. See also page 74 above.

Michels, Robert, *Der Patriotismus; Prolegomena zu seiner soziologischen Analyse*, Munich, 1929.

Moffat, Alfred (ed.), *The Minstrelsy of England; a Collection of 200 English Songs With Their Melodies* . . ., London, 1901.

Nettl, Paul, *Mozart und die königliche Kunst*, Berlin, 1932.

Nettl, Paul, *Mozart in Böhmen*, Prague, 1938.

Nettl, Paul, *The Story of Dance Music*, New York, 1947.

Nettl, Paul, *Luther and Music*, Philadelphia, 1948.

Nissen, Nikolaus von, *Biographie W. A. Mozarts*, Leipzig, 1828.

Pan-American Union, *see* Unión panamericana.

Pedrell, Felipe (ed.), *Cancionero musical popular español* . . ., 4 vols., Valls-Cataluña, 1918—1922. See also pages 24, 137 above.

Pohl, Carl Ferdinand, *Joseph Haydn*, 3 vols., volume III completed by Hugo Botstiber, Berlin-Leipzig, 1875—1927. See also page 61 above.

Possel (ed.), *Taschenbuch für die neueste Geschichte*, Music Supplement, Nuremberg, 1798. See also page 74, above.

Pottier, Eugène, *Chants révolutionnaires*, Paris, 1887. See also page 129 above.

Rousseau, Jean Jacques, *Dictionnaire de musique*, Paris, 1768. See also pages 4, 10, 11 above.

Rychnovsky, Ernst, *Smetana*, Stuttgart, 1924.

Sachs, Curt, *Eine Weltgeschichte des Tanzes*, Berlin, 1933. See also page 31 above.

Scheurleer, Daniel François, *Het Muziekleven in Nederland in de tweede helft der 18ᵉ eeuw* . . . . 's Gravenhage, 1909.

Schirmer, Robert, *see* Treharne, Bryceson.

Schmid, Anton, *Joseph Haydn und Nicolo Zingarelli*, Vienna, 1847. See also page 56 above.

Slonimsky, Nicolas, *Music of Latin America*, New York, 1945. See also "Index" *s.v.* Slonimsky.

Sonneck, Oscar George Theodore, *Report on "The Star-Spangled Banner," "Hail Columbia," "America," "Yankee Doodle,"* Washington, 1909. See also page 172 above.

Spitta, Philipp, *Musikgeschichtliche Aufsätze*, Berlin, 1894.

Sporck, Franz Anton, *Christliche Kinderlehr*, 1721. See also page 92 above.

Tappert, Wilhelm, *Wandernde Melodien*, Berlin, 1889 (2nd edi= tion). See also "Index" *s.v.* Tappert.

Telemann, Georg Philipp, *Der getreue Musikmeister*, 1728. See also page 46 above.

Tiersot, Julien, *Histoire de la Marseillaise*, Paris, 1915. See also pages 74, 75 above.

Tobler, Alfred, *Kühreihen oder Kühreigen, Jodel und Jodellied in Appenzell* . . ., Leipzig, 1890.

Treharne, Bryceson (ed.), *National Anthems of the United Nations and Associated Powers; English Versions of Foreign Texts by Lorraine Noel Finley; Music Arranged and Edited by Bryceson Treharne; Compilation, Historical and Biographical Notes by Robert Schirmer* . . ., Boston, 1943.

Unión panamericana (ed.), *Himnos nacionales de las repúblicas americanas*, Washington, 1949.

Valerius, Adrianus, *Nederlandtsche Gedenck Clanck*, 1626. See also page 91 above.

Vavřik, Jaroslav, *Lidová Písen ve Slezsku Moravske Ostrave,* 1931. See also page 122 above.

Wendel, Hermann, *Die Marseillaise; Biographie einer Hymne,* Zurich, 1936.

Zweifel, Paul, *Über die Schlacht von Sempach zur Aufklärung der Winkelriedfrage,* Zurich, 1927.

INDEX OF FIRST LINES

INDEX

Furnadshiew, Nikola, 225
Fyle, C. Nelson, 150

Gabelli (Italian composer), 108
Gabon, 158
"Galimathias Musicum"
    (Mozart), 94
Galliard rhythm, 45
Gambetta (music teacher), 151
Garibaldi, Giuseppe, 107, 110
"Garibaldi Anthem," see "Inno
    di Garibaldi"
Die Gartenlaube (periodical), 73
Gay, John, 15
Gbeho, Philip, 153
Geffrard, Nicolas, 190
Geibel, Emanuel, 2
Genetz, Emil, 100
Gentleman's Amusement
    (periodical), 209
Gentleman's Magazine
    (periodical), 38
George I (of Great Britain), 48
George I (of Greece), 117
George II (of Great Britain), 38,
    48
George V (of England), 223
German Democratic Republic,
    88
German Federal Republic, 88
Germany, 1, 2, 10, 15, 16, 18,
    19, 29, 52, 79 - 90, 107
Gershwin, George, 22
Ghana, 153 - 154
Ghandi, Mahatma, 172

Giménez, Gimberto, 197
"Giovinezza," 107, 108, 109
Gluck, Christoph Willibald, 10,
    11, 15, 20, 28, 56
"God Defend New Zealand,"
    215, 216
"God save the King," 30,
    33 - 47, 48, 49, 53, 60, 68, 73,
    79, 164, 213, 214, 218,
    223 - 224
Goethe, Johann Wolfgang von,
    22, 54, 75, 78
Golde (German composer), 85
Gossec, François Joseph, 74
Gounod, Charles François,
    19, 110
Gradenwitz, Peter, 138
Granados Campina, Enrique, 20
Great Britain, 16, 29, 31,
    34 - 51, 101, 205, 214
The Great Elector of Rathenow
    (Rambach), 43
Greece, 117 - 118; Ancient
    Greece, 1
Grétry, André Ernest Modeste,
    74, 75
Greulich, Wilhelm, 84
Grieg, Edvard, 103
Griepenkerl, Robert, 78
Grigorios, Patriarch, 117
Grillparzer, Franz, 61, 62
Grimm, Baron Melchior von, 10
Griots aux Morts, 147
Grison, Jean-Baptiste Lucien,
    74, 75